Master Plant Teachers

Master Plant Teachers

Entheogens Facilitate Mystical Experiences

Nancy Clark, Ph.D

From the author of *Our Divinity Revealed*

KNOW THYSELF AS DIVINITY

Published by

Dr. Nancy Clark, Ph.D. Publishing | nancyclarkphd.com

Publisher's Cataloging-in-Publication Data
Clark, Nancy.

   Master plant teachers : entheogens facilitate mystical experiences / Nancy Clark. – Flagler Beach, FL : Nancy Clark, PH.D. Pub., 2023.

   p. ; cm.

   ISBN13: 978-0-9601187-4-8 (softcover)
   978-0-9601187-5-5 (hardcover)

   1. Hallucinogenic drugs and religious experience. 2. Spiritual life. I. Title.

   BL65.D7 C53 2023

   204.2--dc23

Project coordination by Jenkins Group, Inc. | www.jenkinsgroupinc.com

Printed in the United States of America
27 26 25 24 23 • 5 4 3 2 1

To Divine Source, who goes by thousands of names.
The pathway to you is love.
You dance to the delight in many forms.
Creation is unique expressions of you.
Your Divine Essence is hidden within,
but wise are those who recognize you.
O Beloved, the recognition of Source within
are those who are lost in your love.
We are together everywhere, like the wave and the ocean.

Contents

Acknowledgments

I would like to thank Divine Source for this unique expression of life and the ability to serve the Divine Plan. I would like to express my gratitude to all the people who have come into my life who have reminded me of my true identity, without whom this book would not have been possible. So many teachers who had something to add and cause the remembrance, including the Master Plant Teacher, Mother Ayahuasca. I want to honor so many beautiful Souls who have walked along with me, some for a short while and others for much longer. I applaud you, brave Souls, for coming into this world to understand more deeply your true identity as a piece of Source by experiencing the illusion of separation.

Introduction

We are spiritual beings having the human journey. We come here for several reasons, and some of them are to know our true identity and to have the awareness of why we are here, our lessons, and our purpose work, to name a few. We are here to also enjoy being in physicality and experiences along the way yet being aware of our divinity. How do we show up in the world? We need to step deeper into our true energetic signature. It is a state of beingness. We need to be bold and live from the heart. We need to go out each day and be ourselves. Go be ourselves. Let us be our truest expression to the world, to drop into and be our true energetic signature, which is a beingness. Our true beingness is our truest Self. It's a way of being. We have to be it and not just say it. It takes strength, heart, and boldness. Walk each day, being ourselves. The world is waiting for us to be comfortable with ourselves, being ourselves. This is an energetic way of showing up in the world. How we hold ourselves, our uniqueness. The lighthouse does not run all over the land looking to save the boats; it just stands there and shines. We came here not only to step into our purpose work but also to remember our true identity before we stepped into our human form. Entheogens offer this remembering.

Why are so many people from around the world turning to entheogens, also known as psychedelics? Entheogens offer the ability for people to have mystical experiences that show them while in sacred ceremony their true identity, their energetic form, their purpose work, their lessons here on Earth, guidance with current situations in their life, connection with loved ones on the other side of the veil of forgetfulness, spiritual awakening, and so much more. These entheogens are nonaddictive psychoactive substances, and shamans are highly trained for many years to utilize these plants in sacred ceremonies. Shamans are the society of people using plants as a means to successfully have mystical experiences leading to enlightenment, cosmic consciousness, Self-Realization, and God Realization, which all leads to Oneness.

"Psychedelic" comes from the Greek word "psyche," meaning "Soul," which peels back the psyche to reveal the Soul and deeper meanings and revelations. If a person doesn't show respect for the Plant Medicine (this intelligence, this consciousness), then they won't have the experience. It won't happen. The person must adhere to the required diet before the ceremony; the intention, purity, and surrender for this are very special. The gut is full of neurons. What a participant eats will affect their ceremony. The fix is not in the plant medicine brew cup. It's in the integration after the ceremony. The integration process is taking what is revealed to the initiate during the ceremony and bringing this guidance into the person's life, which actively changes in a positive way how a person lives their daily life.

Entheogens allow one to step outside the normal mental activities of the conscious mind and go into other areas in the cranium, such as the pineal gland. Entheogens offer healing and spiritual awakening. Entheogens can offer the ego death, cosmic consciousness, self-realization, and God Realization. Entheogens will provide a different experience for each person. The entheogen can show areas deeply hidden, such as deep grooves in the conscious mind, patterns, habits, and personality issues, to the person while in ceremony or under the influence of the different entheogen substances. Inner experiences are valid and confirmed, and the inner knowing that takes place helps the person make the necessary adjustments. Just taking the entheogens is the first step; then one needs to go into integration and do the inner work needed for a permanent transformation. These inner experiences are never forgotten, and integration helps sort the messages that came through for the person to help with guidance, self-awareness, purpose work, healing, and a deeper connection with the Divine.

The purpose of this book is to show readers that entheogens facilitate mystical experiences. Master Plant Teachers in the form of sacred ceremonial plant medicines and other forms of natural and nonnatural psychedelics allow for people to cross over the veil into higher dimensions and have direct mystical experiences offering insights and bringing people to a higher knowingness of their true identity and Oneness with God. These mystical experiences expand peoples' consciousness to evolve after experiencing Enlightenment, Cosmic Consciousness, Self-Realization, Samadhi, God Realization, and many other dynamic impressions while the inward psychedelic journey is taking place. These mystical travels are outside of time and space, causing a deeper impact; therefore, the Psychonauts are forever changed and introduced to a higher version of themselves.

CHAPTER 1

The Power of Entheogens

Entheogens, also called psychedelics, are naturally and chemically produced substances that originate from plants and are used for greater self-awareness, healing, and spiritual awakening, providing a new way of looking at life. Entheogens allow the ego, mind, personality, and body to step aside and allow the soul to connect in higher dimensions for a variety of experiences. "Entheogen" is a newer word used in place of "psychedelic," in order to differentiate their use as medicines. This removes the stigma associated with the term "psychedelics," which helps people give the proper respect and honor to these plant teachers. Entheogens produce altered states of consciousness or mystical states going beyond the third dimension, into spiritual realms, into the mysterious, metaphysical, or otherworldly. They can lead to a transpersonal or transcendent experience. These substances contain psychoactive components; when used in a spiritual, mystical, and ceremonial environment, they produce an experience beyond that of our default world perceptional experience.[1]

In the psychedelic and Indigenous communities, there is a knowing that the plants were placed on the planet before humanity, so they could help and heal humans. "In my own experiences, these sacred plant medicines have helped me heal intergenerational trauma, to find peace with deceased loved ones, and to look at my own life and improve many areas of it." The Indigenous people from many South

American countries use Ayahuasca as a religious ceremony, and the brew is very sacred; the elixir provides communion with the Divine Essence that pervades everything. In Mexico and with the Native American tribes, peyote is the sacred medicine to help with healing emotionally, as well as physically, and it provides deep spiritual connection with the Infinite Essence within all. Psychedelic research over the years has found the benefits of utilizing the sacred plant medicines in mental health and medical arenas. The current research treatments are mostly in mental health areas, yet pharmaceutical companies are currently doing research and trying to create synthetic versions of the different plant medicines in order to purchase patents for mass distribution to the public in the future. There is concern about "psychedelic capitalism" and what it will do to the Indigenous communities being exploited by the mass demand of these sacred plants that have been used by these native communities for thousands of years. These plants are sacred and have spiritual powers, for they cause awakening to take place during religious ceremonies and are not meant to be used for capitalistic purposes. Yes, they will help globally, yet mass harvesting will drive them into extinction. There needs to be replanting of these sacred plants, and preservation measures need to be taken very seriously. Currently, the Amazon is being exploited, and psychedelic plants are harvested without any seeding of new plants. People are going deeper and deeper into the South American jungles and cutting down every psychedelic plant and vine they can find and selling them to the highest bidder. This is the concern of the Indigenous communities, where there is no respect for these Master Plant Teachers who are willing to help at the risk of extinction, yet focus needs to be taken in the horticultural care of them. There is a religious belief by the Indigenous people that to thank the plant for giving up its life, an offering is given to the sacred plant; this is known as "sacred reciprocity," which lovingly gives respect and honor to the blessed plant. People and corporations are purchasing the lands that hold these sacred plant medicines and pushing the Indigenous communities off their land that they have been living on for hundreds or thousands of years. We are seeing a "colonial and racialized Western mentality" that continues to devastate these Indigenous communities, for they don't have the funds to pay for large legal fees to fight against these huge corporations or wealthy individuals that purchase hectors of land from the South American governments. The plants are the life givers, and now they are in need of protection from capitalism.[2]

Entheo is a Greek word meaning "god within" and is used in connection with entheogens because it allows one to have that Mystical Oneness with the Divine Source. It shows our transparency, without all the coverings of the emotional, mental, and physical bodies, to show our true divine nature, which is our soul made of Source Frequency. The last portion of the entheogen word is "*gen*," to mean "becoming"; therefore, our mystical experience of entheogens would cause an awakening of the revelation that God is indeed within us and our becoming these likenesses of the Divine. Entheogens provide "vision-producing drugs," and these sacred plants are celebrated by being on this planet. Entheogens impart mystical experiences during sacramental ceremonies. Entheogens include natural and nonnatural psychedelics that allow participants to cross the veil into other spiritual realms and have direct mystical experiences bringing insights and a knowingness of their true identity and oneness with God.[3]

The meaning of entheogens is being called to be more relevant, as in "Discovering God within" to be a closer description of what a participant discovers when going inward during an entheogenic session.[4] Ecstasy is closely related to the word "shamanism" because of shamans' ability to create this experience between the entheogenic plants and humans. The shaman offers an opening to allow the sacred plant teachers to communicate with the humans to experience ethereal realms outside of conscious reality. There is a reverence by the shaman toward this Divine Essence that is in these psychoactive plants, for they allow entrance to other realms. These psychotropic plants existed on this planet long before humans lived on this earth. Modern scientists and doctors try to speculate, yet a highly trained shaman knows these transcendent realms. It is the Vegetalista shaman that connects telepathically to the different plants, and this relationship is cultivated over many years. Of course, scientists and doctors are perplexed as to the hidden intelligence of plants, for they have not developed a relationship with the plant kingdom and only want to grind them up, place them in a capsule, and sell them for financial gain. Plants want to help humanity, yet the shamans say that the plant spirit leaves when in the clinical laboratory setting. The vegetalista shaman sings *icaros* (songs of reverence) to the plants while they are harvesting them, while they are cooking them, and while they are in sacred ceremony. Otherwise, the healing does not take place, for it has to do with the shaman's training and relationship with the plants.[5]

Around the world, psychoactive plants grow, and for millennia people have ingested them. We have artwork of psychedelic mushroom carvings in Mexico, Central America, Spain, Bulgaria, and Algeria. There are documented customs of entheogenic mushroom use from thousands of years ago in Siberia, India, Scandinavian regions, Lithuania, Greece, and many Indigenous cultures. There is the iboga psychotropic plant in Africa and the psychospiritual entheogenic medicine plant ayahuasca from the Amazon areas. Peyote cactus with a psychedelic substance was and still is used by North American Native Indians and Indigenous tribes in Mexico and South America. In India, the plant Soma was so revered because of its psychedelic properties and ability to create mystical experiences that the Hindu priest class in India declared it a deity for its ability to show Divinity Within. These sacred entheogenic plants are a blessing placed upon the earth. There is even Christian artwork from the early century AD showing Jesus and early saints in many churches with psychedelic mushrooms providing self-inquiry, expansion of consciousness, and remembrance that one is an Infinite Soul.[6]

A highly trained shaman deals with the spiritual aspects of the participants in their ceremonies or works with individuals separately. Illness and disease are a spiritual imbalance and need correction by healing from traumas, which will also heal any physical ailments. For centuries all shamanistic Indigenous cultures have been working in the spirit realms to help Souls in their human journey. Shamans also see the spirits that exist in all forms of life, and this is why they enjoy not only helping humanity but also working with the plant, animal, and bird kingdoms that come to them.[7] The name "shaman" doesn't exist in the Amazon culture; they go by different names such as vegetalista (because they work with different types of plants) and curandero. Some plants are for healing, and others are for awakening and spiritual growth.[8]

On this planet, shamanism is the most ancient esoteric wisdom for humanity. The Indigenous cultures existed long before modern societies and had to rely on the consciousnesses of the plants, animals, and birds for their wisdom. Modern societies are only beginning to realize and appreciate the spiritual truths from what they perceived incorrectly as "primitive cultures" and are starting to incorporate these healings into modern Western life. It was a matter of survival in ancient times for Indigenous communities living among and in natural environments to accept the help of these Master Plant Teachers, the master animal teachers, and the master bird teacher. Modern humans have stepped away from the natural environment and therefore lost the connection with these esoteric wisdoms that the plants, animals, and birds hold within and who are willing to share them to awaken the sleeping humanity. We are fortunate to still have Indigenous communities on this planet and to garner their wisdoms in how to live and provide healing. Shamanic cultures are oral traditions in which they pass down their knowledge to the next generation and through direct teaching of the different ways to communicate in ordinary and non-ordinary realities. Due to the overwhelming demand asking for help from modern individuals, the shamanic people are sharing their wisdoms to help humanity on this planet. Modern societies have much to garner from the shamanic way of life, which is in balance and harmony with all life that lives on this planet.[9]

Shamans have certain techniques for the ability to travel into spirit worlds to provide healings, bring back messages, and help participants connect with the etheric dimensions. There is only a thin veil between the physical reality and the ethereal realities. The lower worlds are in the center of the Earth with a portal that connects to the upper realms. There can be scenes of darkness and lower beings on an entheogenic participant's journey in the beginning, and then they move beyond these to a more beautiful scenery and celestial essence dimension where messages can be accessible. The center of the Earth is the first dimension that is visited, and then a participant travels beyond onto the cosmic realms in the universe, then further onto a paradisiacal realm filled with transcendental mystical experiences. The shamans have access to and offer an opportunity to travel to these different levels of realities.[10]

Shamans require years of training, and they perform a number of functions for humanity. The shaman is able to communicate with the spirits in the spirit world, treat illnesses related to negative spirits, go on visionary quests, and ask spirit guides for answers. They cross the veil to work with animal guides and elementals, such as fairies and other mythical beings, to bring back messages, and they have special abilities to cross the veil that separates the spirit world from the physical world. Spiritual dimensions do exist, according to shamans all over the world, and their specialty is traveling and working in these other dimensional realities. We know of the elementals because many people have traveled to these etherical realms and have seen them, interacted with them, and experienced them directly. Many people will say they are mythical, yet that is because they do not exist in this physical reality. They do exist in a more ethereal reality, because people such as shamans and entheogenic participants have traveled to these other realities, interacted with them, and come back into this physical reality to share of these beings. In order for a person to become a shaman, there is a multitude of approaches to the selection process, and temperament is one of the many characteristics that an older experienced shaman will look for before mentoring a future shaman to go into shamanistic training.[11]

Women also become powerful shaman and healers. In most cases, after the child-raising years are completed, some women in

Indigenous cultures will train to become shamanic healers. There is no difference between men and women in the ability to become a shaman. Women are more intuitive by nature and therefore have a greater potential to become master potent healers. In the Middle Dark Ages, women who practiced shamanic healing modalities were declared "witches" by the Christian Vatican belief system. Many were murdered or burned for fear they were working against the Vatican Christian Church beliefs. Once a shaman reaches a certain level, psychic powers are also achieved with the shamanic healing abilities. Master-level shamans around the world are able to see what is taking place currently with modern societies on this planet through the psychic ability of clairvoyance. This is why shamans are reaching out to help humanity awaken to the reality that we share this planet with all living beings in different physical forms and all is made of the Infinite Divine Essence.[12]

Having an experienced guide is most important when entering unearthly realms. A master guide will know the different spiritual dimensions and provide protection if a guest traveler encounters difficulties. From youth, a shaman is trained, then internship starts for additional years under the guidance of a master shaman to show the ability to travel and learn the ethereal territories and the possible dangers of these extra-dimensional realities. They have to demonstrate their skills as an accomplished guide and an adept healer and communicate with the plant and animal spirits, navigate the different spirit realms and beings that inhabit them, and reach spiritual mastership to have the power to protect the entheogenic participants while on their journey during the sacred plant ceremonies. Currently, in modern societies, people have popped up claiming to be shamans who have no lineage or who have not demonstrated to an advanced master shaman their skills or abilities; they mislead people to think that their entheogenic journeys are spiritually protected and that accurate healings are available.[13]

Shamanism is closely related to the term "ecstasy," which comes from the Greek word *ekstasis,* defined as "to leave the body."

Another expression, "flight of the soul," is used to describe the mystical experience. It is the shaman who is well trained in these ecstatic states of consciousness. The shaman calls upon the plant spirits to help while traveling in the upper and lower dimensions. Between the shaman and the plant spirits, they navigate through the different dimensions. A well-trained shaman will be able to work with the Master Plant Teachers, who are the entheogenic plants, which allow for the consciousness of the participant to leave the body and travel into the different dimensions. The sacred Plant Teachers were seen as gods in the ancient cultures for their ability to change the participants' perception of themselves and the world around them. These entheogenic plants had the power to expand one's consciousness, which is why they were held in such high esteem and considered God-like in nature for their transcendent abilities. There will always be shamans on this planet to help humanity in their evolution and awakening process with the aid of entheogenic plants that provide the psychospiritual medicine.[14]

Shamans work in the spirit realms; they map these territories and come to know them very well, since they spend many travels in them. Time has no meaning or place in these spirit realms. The nature spirits come out to say hello to the shaman while on their missions. These spiritual realms are magical, for animals are able to fly and vegetation talks to the shaman. A master shaman is able to utilize these ethereal helpers for guidance, help, and protection while journeying in these upper and lower realms.[15]

There is a close relationship between the shaman and the plants; however, it takes a lot of time to develop this trust and bond between them. The shaman sings *icaros* (songs) to the plants and must participate in the *dieta*, which is a strict diet and lifestyle. This *dieta* seclusion period demonstrates to the plants that they are willing to leave society, go out into the forest, and spend time with the spirits of the plants. *Dietas* are done every so often to keep this connection to commune and communicate with the plant kingdom. During the *dieta*, wisdoms from the plant spirits (plant consciousness intelligence) are shared with the shaman. After a period of time the shaman will come out of retreat with the plants and go back into the village or society to perform sacred plant ceremonies. People in the modern world can no longer hear the plants sing to them. They are too consumed by modern technology, removed from nature, and no longer connected to the plant kingdom. When an entheogen is introduced into a person's body, the Default Mode Network in the brain is reduced so the participant can disengage from the ego and connect with other dimensional realities within them.[16] The plants and flowers know exactly how to communicate with the nervous system and emotions of humans. The plants know what is needed, and communication is provided, for there are receptors in the brain that recognize all plant essences and are waiting for these messages. The intelligence of the plant cells has the ability to communicate directly with the human cells.[17]

During the sacred entheogenic plant ceremony, the shaman raises their vibration to a high frequency of energy so they have the power to see into the future, the past, and currently what is taking place in the participant's life. There are different levels of shaman that allow the ability to have this dominion over the physical world. The two highest levels are banco sumi and sumiruna, and once a shaman reaches these two levels, they have the privilege of the abilities to see beyond this third-dimensional reality. We do have celestial beings walking this planet in the form of banco sumi—level shamans. The incarnated celestial beings become banco sumi shaman in order to heal and help humanity. The sumiruna are souls that are humans who have risen their vibration high enough to achieve this level of sumiruna shaman. An eagle in the shamanic cultures is a representation of humans' ability to rise above the human weaknesses and accomplish self-mastery of divine spiritual truths.[18]

There is a state of consciousness that the shaman specifically uses for their work in the spiritual realms. This shamanic state of consciousness provides the shaman the ability to travel to different territories to perform the work that is needed to help the individuals who come to them for healing. There are realms that are so spectacular and others that are very dark. Master shamans travel frequently to these different areas and know how to navigate the dangers and powers.[19] After an entheogenic experience, it is reported that many change their life due to the esoteric nature of the exploration event. Plant life, animals, and, in fact, all of life seem to take on more meaning and significance—a new way of living in the world that offers living in greater harmony so as not to hurt other living species on this planet. Most people, when first exposed to the idea of Master Plant Teachers, will not take it seriously, yet ask any Indigenous people around the world, especially the vegetalista shaman, and they will tell you straightforwardly that plants are sentient beings and within the plant kingdom there are Plant Teachers who are here to help humanity to awaken. The awakening of humanity would cause peace, harmony, and unity as well as an increase in spiritual awareness that will save not only humans but also all of life living here and the planet itself. All species want to live without harm and enjoy their life. Entheogens foster ecological responsibility and an appreciation for nature.[20]

The Hopi Indians know that all has life in it. In Hopi tradition, some humans pretend they are birds, rivers, animals, and so forth. If a human disguised as a plant, bird, tree, or animal is killed, then they don't return to the human world. The killed, being in future generations, will come in and take a role as living in this physical reality as a plant, bird, tree, animal, and so on. We all are part of the same Creator Source and share the same creative life force. The Hopi Indians look upon a bird, animal, and plant as humans disguising themselves and having another life as a human in ordinary reality. We could be a fairy, unicorn, leprechaun, or more, enjoying these magical experiences in nonordinary states of consciousness, while in our waking state of ordinary consciousness having the human experience. This is what the Hopi Indians believe and see occurring when they travel these spiritual realms. This is why the Hopi Indians say everything is alive and to be kind to all plants, rocks, trees, animals, and all that is seen in this world.[21]

Humanity needs to live in balance with the natural world, to live and share resources with all living beings on this planet. When modern people come into Indigenous cultures, they disrupt the way these people have lived for thousands of years. The exposure to the Western way of living causes Indigenous people to become unbalanced, and greed starts to enter their hearts, hence the participation in cutting down and selling so much of the Amazon plants, herbs, vines, trees, and other natural resources in demand from the Western world. The Indigenous people can lose their connection with nature and their spiritual awareness. Indigenous people are misunderstood to be uneducated and simple, yet they are taught to accept all other ways and beliefs of other cultures, for they see us all as part of the human family. The shamanic cultures teach the honor and protection of all living beings on the Earth.[22]

Plant-based entheogens have been used for thousands of years, and medical researchers are not acknowledging this fact. Any documented information prior to modern times seems to be viewed as irrelevant. Entheogens have been proven and used all around the world for millennia to heal mental, emotional, and physical ailments. Shamans who are well trained specialize in these areas and are considered legitimate healers. Western science is still trying to catch up to the deeper wisdoms of plant intelligence and all the botanical apothecary that is available to humanity.[23]

The vegetalista shaman knows that hidden wisdoms are shared by the plants. As far back as antiquity, Plato, Aristotle, and Sophocles were participants of sacred plant entheogenic ceremonies and were given many esoteric wisdoms that helped shape Greek culture. The mystery schools had entheogenic plant ceremonies as initiations into the esoteric wisdoms. These initiates learned that the plants will talk with them and will allow travel to different realms. Plants also help us in curing disease, they provide nourishment, and they are excellent teachers.[24]

An important aspect of any psychospiritual medicine, especially ayahuasca, is the icaros, which are songs sung by the vegetalista shaman. Each song has its meaning and power. Some icaros are for protection, calmness, guidance, and much more, depending on what is needed by the ceremony participants. These icaros are very special and received only by vegetalista shamans. There are geometrical patterns to each icaro song sung by the vegetalista shaman. Different geometrical patterns correspond with different qualities in which each unique icaro song is sung and placed energetically into each sacred medicine ceremonial participant by the vegetalista shaman.[25]

Vegetalista shamans connect with many plants, yet there will be one in particular that they will bond with, and it will be one of the Master Plants Teachers. This will cause a bond between the plant teacher and the vegetalista shaman by means of dreams, visions, messages, and even direct telepathic communication. A strict diet and disciplines are required during a period of seclusion called a dieta, which lasts usually for at least one month and can last for several months. During the dieta period, the person training to be a shaman or an experienced shaman reconnecting with the plants will be alone in a wooden cabin in the forest away from all distractions, connecting with the plants, receiving initiations from the Plant Teachers, learning to communicate with them, traveling in and out of different dimensions. While in many plant ceremonies over the course of time in the dieta program, these dietas are for training as a new shaman or continuing education for an experienced shaman. The Plant Teachers will become jealous if ignored or if the vowed agreements are not honored; hence, the need to go into dieta for the shaman's attention is required and expected several times a year. Shamans know that their healing abilities come from these plant spirits. These plants are conscious and have been known to cause shamans emotional and physical issues that have broken their initiation rites, causing the shamans to come back to honor their spiritual disciplines. Once an individual has taken the vows of being a vegetalista shaman, their connection with the Plant Teachers, and to include animal spirits, is sacred. The Plant Teacher spirits will feel betrayed if the shaman's vows are broken, causing the close connection to be removed, thereby creating situations for the vegetalista shaman to see what has happened. Usually, it is an older shaman who realizes that these agreements with the Master Plant consciousness are serious and not to be taken lightly. Each Master Plant Teacher has healing abilities and takes on their own individuality, temperament, and tone. They do not like to be ignored and require attention, causing the vegetalista shaman to talk with them and to give gifts to the Plant Teacher in the form of several items, such as fresh loose tobacco, incense, and songs, to name a few.[26]

The sacred brew of ayahuasca allows the master shaman to see the "avatar angels" protecting the earth. These angels impart supernatural energy to the plant kingdom, and the "maestro shamans can see in their visions the angelic powers at work." Many participants have stated that they have met angelic and galactic beings during their mystical experiences during the ceremonies. "Extraterrestrial ships visit Earth frequently. They come from parallel universes," and shamans learn arcane wisdoms from them.[27]

CHAPTER 2

Ambassadors for the Planet

Plants and fruits are expressing the wish to be eaten with loving respect. Plants appreciate communication between them and the person getting ready to eat them, an honoring to the plant for giving up its life to the human. The vegetables would rather be nourishment for humanity than decay out in the field. The plant kingdom is hopeful that the human kingdom will come to understand that there is an energetic connection between them.[28]

The entheogenic plants are the ambassadors for the planet to help humanity wake up and change their ways that are damaging and eliminating life on Earth. These Master Plant Teachers are trying to influence every human being on this planet to a higher vibrational way of living that promotes and sustains life. With wars, pollution waste, toxic chemicals, deforestation, worldwide animal and bird extinctions, and many more caused by unawake humans, these entheogen Plant Teachers are working as agents toward an evolutional rise in human consciousness. The human ego is self-consumed and causing so much damage to all living beings on this planet. Many entheogenic participants are told that things need to change and all of life is calling for the mass awakening in human consciousness. Living with the mentality that everything is disposable and about convenience causes a lifestyle that shows us where we are today with environmental problems, pain, suffering, and loss of life for untold amounts of living beings on Earth.[29]

The cultural environment of the 1960s in the United States was in turmoil. There was the antiwar movement against the Vietnam War; there was the sexual revolution since the birth control pill was released to the public; there was the civil rights movement where African Americans wanted to be treated as equals, as they should be, in a society where the laws were in favor of white Americans; and then there were the psychedelics that were causing people to drop out of corrupt systems and allowing for them to see through the corruption, lies, and deception of the political arena. The psychedelics and the entheogens provided freedom of expression, deep mystical insights, and cultural changes. The United States government had to find a way to control the people—hence the media campaign against psychedelics stating lies about how these psychoactive plants and nonnatural psychedelics were addictive and toxic and the banning of them by making them illegal. The Controlled Substances Act was passed in 1970 by politically motivated lawmakers wanting to remove this opportunity for people to explore their inner environment, who were not wanting to be manipulated by staying in a false, deceptive outside narrative. All the plant-based entheogenic medicine was included in the Schedule 1 level, which is viewed as the most dangerous in the Controlled Substances Act of 1970. Still today they are listed at this Schedule 1 level. It seems interesting that plant-based, consciousness-expanding entheogens are considered the most dangerous on this planet and therefore are illegal and a person will be jailed for using them. What is the mainstream establishment afraid of regarding entheogens? These Sacred Plant Teachers are here to heal our social, mental, physical, and emotional pain, to bring us back into balance and harmony with our planet, and to show us our Divine nature. Shamanism began to appear of interest again in the 1980s. Since then, pharmaceutical companies created ibogaine from the iboga plant, and mescaline comes from the peyote cactus plant, which has therapeutic usages. Shamanism has emerged to share this psychospiritual medicine and to offer opportunities to humanity for healing. The Sacred Plant Teachers are helping humanity to become more balanced, free, and awakened to the true reality of our multidimensionality by experiencing the many dimensions within. Now we see many research projects taking place around the planet, since the entheogens are healing humanity in many essential areas.[30]

Why are some drugs legal and others not legal and forbidden? All drugs will alter brain activity. The legal drugs that are massively produced and available for public use create huge profits for the companies that have patented them and have legal protection. Natural botanicals that come from Mother Earth are free for the public to use and are not able to be patented. Therefore, manufacturers create a synthetic version of the botanical plant, flower, fungi, and so on. Synthetic drug companies don't like competition to their synthetically created drugs. Consequently, botanical drugs were classified as illegal, and these plant wisdom keepers are kept far away from the human population. Why? The synthetic versions came from botanical plants of all kinds. Why are the botanical plants with the ability to expand consciousness the ones that are banned and illegal? Why are the synthetically manufactured drugs produced with all the negative side effects classified as safe for the public? It is interesting that the natural botanical psychotropic plants are nontoxic and have no lasting side effects and have proven themselves over thousands of years of usage by Indigenous cultures around the world for physical, psychological, and spiritual healing. They are available in nature, and the public is denied access. Why is it outlawed to take botanical entheogenic plants that heal and elevate human consciousness? It is a human right to have access to psychospiritual medicine. Research has revealed that the human brain is a transmitter and a receiver. The psychoactive properties within the plants change the wavelength patterns that are received by the neurotransmitters in the brain, offering communication with spiritual beings in other realms. For thousands of years shamans have always said that there is spiritual significance with plant-based entheogens, and the connection is available with these spiritual beings in different dimensional realms.[31]

Personal freedom comes from blazing your own trail. A shaman does not work in a hierarchal spiritual system. The shaman has respect for the master shaman teacher yet does not continue to lord over the accomplished graduated student shaman. Shamanism is a pathless path to find the wisdom within. Paths are only a stepping-stone to bring one to learn higher ideals and teachings. At some point, on a Soul's journey, there comes a time when they are ready to move beyond belief systems into deeper hidden wisdoms. This causes the journey to leave these well-trotted paths and take a path less traveled. The beginning of a pathless path can be difficult and unknown, yet the Soul needs to find this reconnection with Source. This journey is inward, and few are able to teach, prepare, and encourage others to receive these inner wisdoms and inner truths. Personal freedom provides this ability to set sail and explore one's inner dimensions. This is also a paradox, for many times it also takes inner exploration to receive the personal freedom and illumination. This usually comes with a sacrifice where one has to step outside of normal societal boundaries, yet the Soul is ready to remember its true identity as an aspect of Source. Time spent in the lower worlds; the Soul has forgotten that it is spiritual royalty.[32]

A person can have a diminishing of or theft of their life force energy, which can happen in many ways. A highly skilled shaman can retrieve the stolen life force energy and give it back to the rightful person to whom it belongs and who was born with this energy originally. This master-level shaman leaves the physical realm and goes into the spiritual realm to retrieve this stolen energy and bring it back to the initial soul. These spiritual realms are filled with complexities and potential dangers to the shaman, who has to navigate carefully, as not to get trapped or take on any entities. Usually, the stolen soul energy is in the middle and lower planes when going in to retrieve it for the first soul that was born with their soul life force energy. This stolen energy is usually taken by adults while the soul is a young child, since children have so much light and high energy about them. Most of the time, the theft of energy occurs by a parent, teacher, relative, or someone who has access to the child who feels drained of energy due to adult responsivities. There can be a lot of energy removed or a small portion, yet this drains the child, and then sickness, dullness, depression, and so forth come to the individual soul, for only a small amount that is needed to just barely sustain life is left. Soul Retrieval or Life Force Retrieval is needed in order for the individual to have the wholeness of their energy back and to feel fully energized and alive again. Why do you think children are preyed upon so much in society? Children are so full of light and life force energy, and it is desirable. Children are not savvy enough to be able to withstand the psychic attacks and will give in to gain acceptance and love from those around them. Even adults are open prey if not aware of this occurrence that can take place in them. Soul Retrieval/Life Force Retrieval is a long training process for any shaman who takes on this work to help heal humanity.[33]

Shamans are all trained in rituals, yet a master shaman is a deep healer of intrusion who believes that all illness is a result of negative spiritual intrusions into the physical body, only manifesting outwardly what has transpired inwardly. Trauma, betrayal, rape, PTSD, emotional and mental health crises, physical diseases, and so on are a result of a negative spiritual intrusion. Shamans will have many "spirits" helping them in their work, such as plants, animals, birds, and nature spirit consciousnesses from different spiritual realms.[34]

There is outer space, and then there is inner space. In the ancient Buddhist *Udanavarga* texts Buddha talked about what he saw on the inner planes regarding the cosmos. We are spending billions of dollars on space technology to answer questions that have already been answered thousands of years ago and even documented in these ancient texts: "then you have the Buddha, or the Psychonaut, using the inner space station to get the same information." The scientists should be researching the ancient texts that have documented galaxies and these yugas of time that can shed light on this local universe, which has already been mapped by the historical esoteric mystics.[35]

A curandero/vegetalista works with plants, and in the Western world, people call them a shaman; however, they also work with the spirit world. Shamanism has to do with the belief system, rites, and rituals of intelligence with the spiritual world.[36] There is a range of time to which shamanism goes back, and many state that this started as far back as the Paleolithic time period of at least 40,000 years, yet no one knows for sure, and it could be even further.[37] The icaros are the songs that the curandero sings, which provide the communication between the spirit world and the physical world. The spirit of the Master Plant Teacher will instruct to the curandero/vegetalista where the illness is located in the participant's body. The Indigenous people found out because the plants sang to them and told them how they could help and heal them. The icaros comes from centuries of historical curanderos working with the sacred plant medicines. The entheogens are sacred plant medicines that have been used since the dawn of humanity.[38]

There always needs to be a person with the participant who is fully trained and would feel safe while on an entheogen journey. All dangers should be removed and not in the area where the entheogen ceremony will take place. The atmosphere needs to be energetically cleared and purified in and around where the sacred ceremonies are held and experienced by the participants. The shaman needs to be fully trained and have a lot of ceremonial knowledge of dosage levels. This will ensure a safe entheogenic journey for the participants.[39] Shamans, ayahuasqueros, and vegetalismo are also called Vegetalists for their work with plants. Mother Ayahuasca is a consciousness that exists in the entheogenic plants, which are called "plant teachers" and talk with people under their influence.[40] Ayahuasca is created by taking the vine called *Banisteriopsis caapi* and the leaves of *Psychotria viridis* and placing them together in a pot with water and boiling until all the water is removed. While this all-day process takes place, the shaman is singing prayers and blessings over the ayahuasca mixture. Both the *Banisteriopsis caapi* vine and the *Psychotria viridis* leaves contain dimethyltryptamine, which is a psychedelic substance, also known as DMT.[41]

Ayahuasca is the mother of the plant kingdom and heals humans of their sicknesses.[42] Another name used in reference to ayahuasca is "the vine of the soul," for it will connect with the participant's Soul to help with what is needed.[43] Some scientists may argue that there is no entity in the entheogen ayahuasca; however, anyone who has ingested the sacred brew that provides mystical experiences to the participants would say they had a spiritual encounter with a Divine Conscious Being. Entheogens will talk with the participants, will show images, and will show the shadow side, weaknesses, and potentials, as well as heal addictions. Entheogens are classified as illegal due to the power of the pharmaceutical industry, which pressed governmental regulators to outlaw them. So here we have sacred botanicals from the earth that expand consciousness, and people are arrested and given a criminal record and viewed as deplorable people. It is the DMT (dimethyltryptamine) that is classified as illegal due to the potency of the evolution of consciousness. After having a mystical experience, the entheogen participant is forever transformed. This personal transformation is the basis for why removal of drug addictions with entheogens works and these most often never come back, even softer addictions, such as sugar, coffee, and smoking.[44]

Ayahuasca is known as the great awakener, for it will show the participant an overall awareness of many areas of their life, so as to be able to see clearly life situations, who they were before they incarnated, and their mission in this life. People have a propensity to go toward items that intoxicate them. Ayahuasca prepares the participant for death since there is usually a fear of this transition from the physical life to the spiritual life. Mother Ayahuasca guides one on their journey in this life. There is a connection of the Native cultures, such as the Amazon Indigenous tribes and the Indigenous people of India and Asian countries with the Buddhist traditions that focus on altered states of consciousness and alternative realities. Spiritual wealth and wisdoms are acquired with exposure to entheogenic medicine, which allows one to stay focused and live with a better sense of peace.[45]

There are mystical experiences that are ongoing even after the entheogen plant ceremony. The Master Plant Teacher Ayahuasca provides "downloads" of information from all levels and on different topics. As a person goes along their day, these epiphanies flow abundantly and instantaneously into the person. It is Mother Ayahuasca talking with her beloved initiate explaining details, going over wisdoms, providing guidance, giving encouragement, forming goals, helping one remember their purpose work agreement prior to incarnation, and showing perspectives from a spiritual multilevel realm overview. This deep contact is possible and does occur for many ayahuasca participants.[46]

Tibetan monks meditate yet also use plants, one of them called Toe also known as datura, to experience expanded states of awareness. The same type of experience happens when a participant ingests an entheogenic plant as when a Tibetan monk takes certain plants to achieve an enhanced state of awareness.[47]

Iboga is a Master Plant Teacher with masculine energy from Africa that has psychedelic properties and originates from the Bwiti tribe and still exists today. The iboga sacred plant has great healing powers and is deeply embedded in the African culture.[48] People have been asking for centuries how the Indigenous natives all around the world knew how to mix all these different plants together and cook them in a special way to extract the DMT into a tea, brew, tonic, or potion, which affects the initiate during the sacred ceremonies. The Indigenous natives all say the same response as to how DMT was discovered: "The natives claim that the plants themselves told them how they should be used." In Africa, the Indigenous natives use iboga leaves for personal use when needed or for when extreme physical labor is required, and then they use a stronger preparation level to be taken by the initiates for sacred ceremonies.[49]

Plants will reveal their wisdoms, and many times it has been mentioned by people over the centuries how the plants sang to them or talked with them and shared with them hidden esoteric information to help humanity. George Washington Carver, who was a famous botanical chemist, explained, "All flowers talk to me and so do hundreds of little living things in the woods. I learn what I know by watching and loving everything." Many shamans have stated this as well, and this is why there is a deep connection between them and the plants.[50]

There is a consciousness in the plants—plant intelligence that speaks to the participant in the sacred ceremony and facilitates the connection with the information and spiritual presence. Each entheogenic ceremony is unique and highly personal for the participant. The plant is the teacher and facilitator to help the participant be connected with this wisdom that is beyond the ego, shadow, personality, and conscious mind and that instead comes from a higher level of awareness. The participant is in a state of awe and wonder at how naturally the entheogenic experience takes place and how it in no way could be prearranged or preplanned.[51]

George Washington Carver once answered to a person emphatic to know about his special magic with plants, "The secrets are in the plants. To elicit them you have to love them enough."[52] On another occasion while George Washington Carver was reaching out to touch a flower, he stated, "I am touching infinity. It existed long before there were human beings on this earth and will continue to exist for millions of years to come. Through the flower, I talk to the Infinite, which is only a silent force."[53]

Nature is alive, and the plants and nature spirits are sentient beings. The African shaman of the iboga plant shares how sacred all living beings are on this planet and all are aspects of God. Communication exists between all forms of life telepathically. The Master Plant Teacher iboga is a plant that is revered as sacred.[54] A concept that was called "Nanna" believes that plants have a Soul, due to the universal nature that Source is within All, seen and unseen. The plants have a direct connection, and when one holds any type of plant, they are holding an aspect of the Divine. Plants have "spiritual nerves" that through the energy of Source Light Frequency are connected to the cosmos and therefore hold great wisdoms.[55]

Master shamans who trained for years and through untold entheogenic ceremonies learn their mastery of healing and power. The shamans' teachers are avatar angels that allow them "to visit other galaxies, such as Andromeda, and other giant stars, such as Antares."[56] There are a lot of false people who are self-proclaiming themselves to be shamans. Most of these self-proclaimed, untrained, or very inexperienced people who claim to be shamans don't understand that there is more than just doing ceremonial work. A highly trained curandero/vegetalista takes many years serving as an apprentice under a seasoned elder to learn about all the different plants, flowers, leaves, vines, and herbs used for healing, not to mention all the plants used for spiritual purposes. Western people wanting to partake of the entheogens need to be aware of the big-business, unethical practices of these people claiming to be so-called trained shamans.[57]

Vegetalista shamans will use specific plants to heal individuals who come to them or in a group setting of a ceremony. Depending upon the vibrational frequency level of a person, the healing will take place in some cases. In extremely low-vibrational people, the plant spirit will not heal them. For people filled with evil who come for healing, the plant spirit does not want to heal them, and it could make them sicker. Therefore, the vegetalista shaman will listen to the plant spirit of each particular plant that has the cure for each type of ailment, in order to know whether it is best to proceed or not with the person requesting healing.[58]

Many Native cultures believe that illness originates from a negative spiritual encounter, sorcery, a person wishing the patient harm or sending negative thought forms to them, or a psychic attack. The plant spirits will talk to the vegetalista shaman to inform about the proper herbs and or psychedelic plants needed in healing the sick person.[59]

Master shamans are trained for years to move from conscious reality to upper and lower realms very easily by their own choice to help individuals in their ceremonies or in one-on-one situations to heal them from what is causing issues for them. Shamans work with the spiritual aspect of illness and its causes. The shamans work in the spiritual realms helping the participants during the entheogenic ceremony, and they can also work in a one-on-one situation for individuals in need of different types of healing.[60]

Plants are sentient and have memory. There was an experiment that proved this by connecting electrodes to a geranium plant, and there were two people who interacted with this geranium. The first person did all sorts of cruel things to the geranium, such as burn its leaves, poke holes into it, pore acid onto it, and cut some of its roots. The geranium reacted to all this torture, and it was recorded on the polygraph test since the plant was connected to the electrodes. The second person was loving and kind to the geranium by treating its burned leaves, placing nutrients into its soil, spraying it with water, talking to the plant, and helping it heal back to its original state. During the entire experiment the geranium was connected to the electrode to record the graphs on paper as to the reactions to everything. The plant was completely healed, and the next level of the experiment continued. Then the cruel person came back into the room, the plant was so scared that the recordings on the graph paper went crazy, and it was very obvious that the plant remembered this mean-spirited person who had tortured it. Then the person who was kind and took care of the plant in order for it to heal came into the room where the plant was and the polygraph paper recordings were smoothed out, and softer lines were showing on the graph paper, which proved that the geranium also remembered the person who nursed it back to health.[61]

Plants provide a good food source for us, and plant medicines provide healings. Plant spirits provide the teachings and talk to the vegetalista shaman in an entheogenic ceremony or in a healing. Whether in a ceremony or in a one-on-one setting, the plants will provide what the participant needs most at that time. The vegetalista shaman listens to the "plant wisdom" in healing settings and in entheogenic ceremonies.[62]

Humanity is unkind and ignorant to the plant kingdom. Humans develop huge cities; remove necessary nutrients; spray and dump toxic wastes into the ground, rivers, and soil; bulldoze hectors of land; damage the ecological system; and so on. Humanity is in a state of amnesia, not realizing that we are headed toward a "catastrophe" and that not respecting the plant kingdom will leave us all sick and hungry.[63]

The nature spirits urge humanity to stop the violations of Natural Law. Removing large acres of the plant kingdom eliminates the habitat for the animals, and therefore they are dying. Can you hear the cries of all the plants and animals that have lost their lives? Humanity has lost its deep connection with the other living beings also here on this planet. The corrupt modern societies that are causing these atrocities can be destroyed by force, just as Atlantis was removed due to its misuse of power. There is an agreement between humans and Gaia (Mother Earth), and people's indifference and unconcern are removing the food and shelter of all other living beings on this Earth. There needs to be a new appreciation and reverence for all living beings in the plant kingdom, bird kingdom, and animal kingdom, for the humans are not the only ones living on this planet who are sentient. We also share the planet with galactic beings visiting us and who also live here. "Some of the flying saucers here live inside the earth; others under water. Some spirit beings live on earth, others come from outer space, but all live as one. When they join together, they appear like a plant."[64]

CHAPTER 3

Ancient and Current Cultures of Social Acceptance

Buddhism first came out of India. Buddha was a Hindu seeking Enlightenment, and after achieving Nirvana, he went on to teach a new way of absorption with the Divine. Indian Buddhism came long before Tibetan Buddhism. Amrita is the entheogenic potion used by Tibetan Buddhism. Soma is the entheogenic elixir used by Indian Buddhism as recorded in the Rig Veda. Amrita entheogenic liquid is seen in artwork being held in cups by the 16-armed Indian god Hevajra.[65] Soma is recorded in the Rig Veda as a plant god that is very sacred to the Hindus. Soma is an entheogenic mushroom with the power to give wisdom and strength. The Rig Veda is a Sanskrit text over 3,500 years old and extremely devotional to the Hindus.[66]

In the ancient Hindu scripture passages, amrita is a psycho-tropic plant ground into a powder, and then water or milk was added to it to create an entheogenic liquid. Amrita is also known as Soma, which is referred to in the Rig Veda as a drink that will show one that they are eternal and live beyond this physical life. Soma was used in Hindu ceremonies, and the Brahmin priest class drank the entheogenic liquid during their religious fire ceremonies. Soma and

Amrita are different names, yet both are plant-based entheogens used in spiritual ceremonies. The ancient Hindus called it Soma, and in Buddhism it is referred to as amrita. "Amrita" is a Sanskrit word with the meaning of "immortality." The entheogenic potion called Amrita, just like Soma, would show the initiate in sacred ceremony of one's Divinity.[67]

Soma, also known as *Amanita muscaria*, is the entheogenic mushroom, which is red with white spots on top of the head. There are scriptures in the Rig Veda discussing the characteristics of the hallucinogenic mushroom.[68] A mushroom called *Psilocybe cubensis* is locally grown in India. There are several varieties of psilocybin psychoactive mushrooms that grow in India. A modern tribe called Santal in the Bihar State region states that they know that the psilocybin mushroom has psychedelic properties.[69] Soma is a sacred religious plant with psychedelic powers that was used in ceremonies in India. Soma originated from Siberian shamans who traveled to India, most likely on a spice route, and brought Soma with them for their religious ceremonies. The Siberian shamans introduced Soma to the local culture in India where they settled and mingled among the people. The Siberian shamans living among the people in India would perform their religious ceremonies, and soma was introduced and accepted into the culture in ancient India. The Rig Veda mentions Soma 120 times in gratitude for this blessed mushroom of godly qualities. Siberian shamans were known for the usage of Siberian mushrooms in their religious ceremonies.[70]

"Soma-Power" expression was used to imply that the psychedelic substance was in the drink and was a powerful ambrosia. An elixir denoting Soma was an entheogenic plant-based drink used for ancient Hindu and ancient Buddhism ceremonies, only in the Buddhist tradition it was called Amrita, yet in both religious ceremonies it was a psychedelic mushroom potion.[71]

The first confirmation of shamans using magic mushrooms dates back to 8000–6000 BCE from carved artistry on a wall in the Tassili cave in eastern Algeria. The cave carving etched into the rock has the shaman holding a bundle of magic mushrooms in each hand. This verified that psychotropic plants were used in ancient cultures.[72]

Many Indian demigods were entheogenic plants that were so sacred that the Indian priests placed them at the level of a deity. In ancient India, the god Rudra is associated with the mushroom *Amanita muscaria*, and then later the god Siva became popular and is connected with the mushroom psilocybin. In Vajrayana Buddhism, mushrooms were used in religious ceremonies. Also, in Mexico tribes, the Psilocybin mushroom was divinity and therefore was a supreme being. To ingest the psilocybin mushroom was to take communion with "God's flesh," allowing the participant to receive this unity. Vajrayana Buddhism mentions feminine demigods named after different entheogens, and a person's experience communing with them causes similar after-effects. It has been confirmed through research that indeed the Hindu and Buddhist religions used entheogens in their initiation ceremonies. Soma, the entheogenic mushroom that was a deity, is recorded in the Rig Veda as far back as 2500 BCE and was brought into India by way of the Spice Route from shamans from Siberia. Soma was so worshipped that it was a blessed privilege to drink this godly potion and enter into a mystical experience. These sacred religious ceremonies ingesting the soma entheogenic god were paramount to the participant in their religious beliefs and offered a firsthand experience of union with the Divine. In the Vedic tradition, Soma is the sacred elixir, and in the Buddhist tradition, Amrita is the holy ambrosia of the gods. Psilocybin was the entheogen utilized in the Buddhist Amrita sacred psychospiritual cordial served during their religious ceremony. A variety of entheogens were used in Tibetan Buddhism, such as flowering plants, mushrooms, psychoactive grasses, and possible ayahuasca due to the ability of trading between countries using the Spice Routes. Entheogens were used in initiation ceremonies to grant "Buddhahood" without the use of other routine spiritual practices to the initiate.[73]

The entheogenic plant called Soma also went by another name, such as Haoma, to mean the watery liquid was removed and therefore was drank as a strong brew in a sacred plant ceremony with reverence. Soma predates the origins of the Zoroastrian religion in Iran. Soma was so beloved that it was officially recognized as a god that came to earth and was venerated by Varuna, who was a Hindu god, according to the Rig Veda texts.[74]

In Buddhism, the goddess Marici is holding an asoka sprig, which is an entheogenic plant known to provide psychedelic experiences. The asoka tree in Buddhism is a holy tree due to its known spiritual powers. These entheogenic plants communicated with the participants and transferred their power to them. The Asoka tree is also called the Kadamba tree, which has been found in a laboratory to have psychoactive properties similar to psilocybin and DMT (dimethyltryptamine) and therefore produces visions and mystical experiences.[75]

On the other side of the veil are realms way beyond this physical reality. A Soul can fly off into these mystical frontiers and meet other divine beings. These magical mushrooms talk with the experiencers and share their divine wisdoms. Don't be fooled that these are merely plants, for these mushrooms will remind one that they are a god in physical form.[76]

Modern-day initiations in Vajrayana Buddhism still call the sacramental drink Amrita to provide an ego death to the initiate. In the past Amrita was an entheogenic mushroom liquid, yet now for several reasons it is purely symbolic and an herbal drink.[77] It has been discovered by ethnobotanists and pharmacologists that there are over 400 religious cultures around the world that have used entheogens to expand consciousness in their sacred ceremonies. Some of them include Soma, the *Amanita muscaria* hallucinogenic mushroom documented in the ancient Rig Veda texts used in the Hindu religion. Other entheogenic sacred plants included Peyote from the North American Indians and Psilocybin by the tribes in Mexico. The morning glory flower is an entheogen that was used by ancient Mexican Aztecs in religious ceremonies. Ayahuasca has been used in sacred religious ceremonies and still is today in South America. Ergot was the sacred and visionary plant utilized annually in religious ceremonies in ancient Greece at the Eleusinian Mysteries temple complex. Iboga is an entheogenic holy plant still used in African religious ceremonies, and ibogaine (the pharmaceutical-grade version) is used in modern cultures today. Soma is an ancient entheogenic mushroom (*Amanita muscaria*) that was used in Hindu religious ceremonies that originated from Siberia with the ancient trade routes that came to India.[78]

There was a couple, the Wassons, who discovered these special mushrooms and submitted them for laboratory analysis to a French biologist, Roger Heim. Gordan Wasson later sent the mushrooms to the laboratory Sandoz to conduct a further study. Albert Hofmann also looked at these unusual mushrooms, and he discovered the psychoactive substances in these Psilocybe mushrooms and called them psilocybin and psilocin. He also performed research and found that the seeds of the flower morning glory also had psychoactive properties and were being ingested by Indigenous people. Albert Hofmann, who discovered the LSD-25 molecule, was saying that LSD should be included with the other psychoactive substances in the plant medicine group. DMT (dimethyltryptamine) was made into synthetic versions called mescaline, ibogaine, and harmine. DMT was also found in the liquid that comes out of the glands and skin of the *Bufo alvarius* toad and carries psychedelic substances, identified as DMT-5 (5-methoxy-DMT). Ayahuasca also carries DMT in the vine and leaves, which when brewed together provide a natural medicine used by Indigenous people for an unknown number of centuries. Another plant, called marijuana, was found in the mid-1960s: one is called tetrahydrocannabinol (THC) and the other is cannabidiol (CBD), which has more properties for healing pain. THC has psychedelic properties, where as CBD marijuana doesn't cause any psychotropic effects.[79]

Psychedelic plants bring about states of consciousness that transcend the conscious mind. The Rig Veda is one of the oldest texts on this planet, and there are many verses and information that mention a holy brew called Soma. Soma had the ability to provide expanded states of consciousness and allowed people to transcend the third-dimensional reality. In the Rig Veda it was mentioned that the initiates would experience a great light or enlightenment and the discovery of God or God Realization. The Persia Zoroastrian Zend Avesta texts are one of the oldest in the world and describe a holy tea called Haoma. In ancient China, the usage of cannabis, also known as marijuana, was documented by the Chinese Emperor Shen Neng from as far back as 2737 BC. It was used for healing, relaxation, and during spiritual ceremonies. It is theorized that entheogens were used in early Jewish times. In the Bible, in the Old Testament, a white substance called manna is mentioned, and many feel it was psychedelic in nature. The Aztecs, Mayans, and Toltecs called the psychedelic mushroom Peyote. There are also seeds from flowers, such as morning glory and angel trumpets, that have psychedelic effects and are currently used, in addition to peyote, for sacred ceremonies by Indigenous natives in Mexico and North American tribes. The Amazonian sacred brew called ayahuasca goes back so far in history that no one really knows when its use began for the South American native tribes. Ayahuasca is known for its healing properties and for spiritual ceremonies. Ayahuasca is known as the plant that will cause an awakening and initiate one to a greater awareness.[80] It has been said by many Indigenous people that the plants told them of the botanical psychedelic properties that would allow the ancient Greeks the ability to cultivate these substances. The plant teachers would have instructed the herbalists in Greece the same way they would have taught the Mexican herbalists, and hence the same psychedelic fungus was seen and experienced in both ancient cultures.[81]

It is believed by William Emboden, an ethnobotanist, that *Datura* and *Nymphaea caerulea* were plant-based entheogens used in Egyptian religious ceremonies. They would have come from the Mediterranean area, dried, and through the ancient spice route be transported to Egypt. Other known entheogens were used in Egypt for medicine and sacred religious ceremonies; they would include ergot (*Claviceps*), mandrake (*Mandragora*), blue lotus (*Nymphaea*), vines (*Vitis*), flowering plant (*Datura*), and opium poppy flower (*Papaver*), plus possible others that are currently unknown. The Acacia tree grew in ancient Egypt and had psychoactive DMT fungus that grew on it. All these entheogenic plants would cause an ego death and rebirth of mystical experiences that Egyptian initiates would have during the religious ceremonies. There is an ongoing list of entheogenic plants being researched and documented that were used in ancient Egypt. It is accepted that entheogens were a prominent part of Egyptian ancient life.[82]

Amanita muscaria was an entheogenic mushroom that was ground up and placed into wine for the initiates to drink, and they also ate the tops of the mushrooms; these practices go back to the Greek religious ecstasy festivals and sacred entheogenic ceremonies of Dionysus (also known as Bacchus).[83] The Mysteries of Eleusis took place annually for the initiates for two millennia in ancient Greece. Then with the rise in power of the early Christian Vatican Church in the fourth century, they deemed it pagan, heretical, and too wicked to continue, and therefore, shortly after the Council of Nicaea decreed, the Eleusinian Mysteries ceremonies closed permanently. The secrecy only added to the mystery of the ceremonies, for all initiates were bound to keep what took place secret and never to reveal the details or their mystical experiences. People came from all over the world to participate in this once-in-a-lifetime experience, for the experiencer could participate in only one sacred ceremony. Each participant would go through only one initiation and therefore only one religious Mysteries of Eleusis ceremony in their entire life. This mystical experience was highly prized, and the only thing that was shared was that it was a personally deep, meaningful spiritual experience.[84]

Kykeon is the mystic elixir that was served to the Eleusis Mysteries participants, which included the ergot, *Claviceps purpurea*, which has psychotropic properties. *Claviceps purpurea*, which is a fungi mushroom species, grew on the local grains and wild grasses in the area near the Eleusis temple complex.[85] A mythical story about the Greek goddess Persephone is that while she was picking flowers, she was abducted by Hades and he took her to a lower spiritual realm where the dead reside.

The type of flower Narkissos would have hallucinogenic alkaloids and is called "Persephone's flower." Plato, who was a recorded initiate of the Eleusis mystical ceremonies, wrote stories of a maiden called Pharmaceia, also known as "use of drugs," in which he alluded to the priest class's usage of psychedelics in the Eleusis ceremonies in Greece. Plato was basically saying in an allegory that Persephone was taken over by ingesting a flower with psychotropic properties and then having mystical experiences. In Greek culture and in many agricultural cultures the "Sacred Marriage" is the union between the spiritual realms and all the vegetation sentient beings on Earth. The spiritual beings dance with the vegetation beings and bring Light, which provides nourishment to plants, which then feed all of life.[86]

It is known in the Eleusinian Mysteries that a holy brew was served to the initiates, and it forever changed how they saw themselves and the external world of appearances. They experienced the ego death and saw that there was no reason to fear a death of their mortal body. This was such a sacred experience. These sacred entheogenic ceremonies stayed in existence for almost 2,000 years. The end of these Eleusinian ceremonies came because of a Christian emperor, Theodosius, who decreed that they must stop and considered them pagan. There was a gigantic hall in Eleusis where over 3,000 initiates could partake in the highly spiritual entheogenic ceremonies at the same time. There were several famous initiates that participated in the Eleusis ceremonies over the 2,000-year time frame, including Plato, Aristotle, the emperor Marcus Aurelius, and the Roman lawyer and consul Marcus Tullius Cicero, who later became a philosopher and reported about how these ceremonies were the cause that shaped civilizations.[87]

In the Eleusinian mythical traditions, death and rebirth were the cycle of life in agricultural societies. The Greek god called Dionysus provided the cultivation of barley and once fermented with a fungus would provide a drink containing hallucinogenic substances. "Clearly ergot of barley is the likely psychotropic ingredient in the Eleusinian potion." In the Greek culture fermented drinks of all kinds were created, made from different plants, fruits, grains, and herbs.[88] The Eleusis Mysteries was an annual event of participants who were initiated in order to have an actual mystical experience. Eleusis was not a spiritual school; it was a once-in-a-lifetime experience. Aristotle, Plato, Sophocles, and others could not break their initiation vows of silence, for death was the penalty, yet they hinted at how glorious it was to have the Eleusis Mysteries experience. Religions today talk about these mystical states of being, yet they don't offer any direct, firsthand mystical experience of connection with the Divine Essence. Anyone who was interested in spirituality and the mystery of life, and who wanted to experience the arcane truths directly for themselves, came to Eleusis to be initiated into the Mysteries. The Eleusis Mysteries lasted for almost 2,000 years and were put to an end by Theodosius, a newly converted zealot Christian who was a Roman emperor. The Mysteries of Eleusis delivered what was promised to the participants, which is why it lasted so long. Each Eleusis initiate would have visions and removal outside of their body to experience their Divine Self and thus their immortality, seeing that there is life beyond this physical plane of existence. The Eleusis Mystery entheogenic potion served to all the initiates was called Kukeon. Once a person was initiated and thereupon went through the mystical experience, they had achieved the designation of *epoptes*, which denotes "the one who has seen it all." The mystical experience forever changed those epoptes who continued on with their lives, became awakened, cracked the riddle of life, and saw their true Divine identity. When the time came for the passing from this physical life, the epoptes were no longer afraid of death, for they had already known what lies on the other side, remembering their True Self identity, which is eternal. It was the entheogen that facilitated this mystical experience for each participant. Before all the major religions of the world, there was Eleusis. The spiritual center for the world was Eleusis, and people came from all over to have the mystical experience that was promised would change their life forever. The entheogenic visionary brew called Kukeon redeemed them from the dream state and awakened them to their Divine nature of immortality.[89]

It was an honor and a once-in-a-lifetime event to be able to be initiated into the Eleusis Mysteries and therefore be included in this religious community. A participant could be initiated only once in their life. The Eleusis initiation was a major part of the Greek culture, and people came from far and wide to be among the participants who encountered these sacred ceremonies. All walks of life came to be initiated into the Eleusis Mysteries; from the top dignitaries, royal families, and political leaders to poets, authors, and teachers of all levels and subjects, as well as slaves and free people, no one was turned down based on economic, civil, or vocational status. The tide turned against these spectacular opportunities that the Eleusis temple offered the population, which was allowed for everyone to experience for almost two millennia. The Christian Vatican Church in the fourth century had become the new official religion in Greece and thus ended the Eleusis ceremonies permanently.[90]

The Ergot of *Claviceps* used in Eleusis ceremonies came from barley and local grasses, not from rye. It is undisputed that the Eleusis potion had an Ergot substance in it and was ingested during the ceremony that created the sovereign and highest point of a spiritual experience. Evidence shows that ergot grew on local grasses in Greece and also on barley grain. Greeks had learned that ergot is a fungus that has psychedelic properties. Rye did not become part of any diet until after the start of the Christian era in 313 AD. The Greek Eleusis ceremonies were ended by the Christian Church decree from Rome shortly after 313 AD.[91] Once someone has a sacred mystical experience, it is hard to put into words, and the initiates of the Eleusinian Mysteries were bound to secrecy. All the information found on what happened in the Eleusis annual religious ceremonies verifies that psychedelic substances were used to facilitate the mystical experience for the participants.[92]

The Eleusis Mysteries were celebrated by thousands of people each year. The Eleusis temple complex was just outside of Athens. Two Eleusis Mystery ceremonies were held twice a year, one ceremony in the spring and the other ceremony in the autumn. During the years that Eleusis Mysteries ceremonies took place, secrecy was kept so prominently that even to this day no one really knows all the complete details of what took place during these sacred plant ceremonies. The Roman statesman Cicero, who as a documented participant of the Eleusis Mysteries ceremony, wrote that individuals from all over the world made a pilgrimage to the Eleusis Mysteries temple for initiation.[93]

The entheogenic mystical experiencer was unable to put into words their Eleusinian ceremony, and therefore this once-in-a-lifetime, precious memory was ineffable. "These are the symptomatic reactions not to a drama or ceremony, but to a mystical vision; and since the sight could be offered to thousands of initiates each year dependably upon schedule, it seems obvious that an hallucinogen must have induced it." Based upon what little the Eleusinian initiates did share, it was a transformational experience.[94] Kykeon was a botanical elixir that was served to the Eleusinian initiate. Soma is a psychedelic served in Indian and Persian religious ceremonies to their participants in order for them to have sacred mystical experiences.[95]

It has been discovered that there is a connection between the Mexican mushroom and the Eleusis Mysteries. The "ineffable visions" are described by the experiencers in both cultures, and mushrooms grew and were traded in the Greek culture. The Greeks have an expression that says "Mushrooms were the food of the gods" and considered holy plants. Mystical experiences were much sought after and experienced by many in the Greek antiquity culture, and they were discussed in the writings from many authors at that time. Plato even discussed how this magical mushroom was capable of providing mystical visions and was able to take one to realms beyond this physical world. Plato's teachings revealed in allegory form the sacred geometric patterns that are part of the mystical experience and many other deep esoteric meanings that only a participant would have learned while in the Eleusis temple during a religious entheogenic ceremony. The Greek word *ekstasis* was the name of the elixir given to the religious initiates during the entheogenic ceremony, and the meaning of the word is "flight of the soul," to explain leaving the body to travel into other realms; this is what this sacred drink offered to anyone who ingested it during the Eleusis Mysteries ceremony. The name of the Mexican mushroom is called "agape of Mexico" and describes the same mystical experiences as the *ekstasis* of the Eleusis ceremonies.[96]

Entheogens are recorded in ancient Greece in Eleusis and in the temple of Hathor in Egypt. We need to realize that because of trade routes all over the ancient cultures, entheogens were readily available. Our modern thinking causes us to believe that ancient cultures did not use psychotropic plants for healing, visions, and religious ceremonies because of the fact that they are not legal and are freely available to the public today. Entheogens were part of the ancient cultures. "Psychedelia was, in many ways, legal in the ancient world… and it is simply historically inaccurate to imagine otherwise." Even the early Christians, who were known as the Nazarenes, and then later called Gnostic Christians, utilized the sacred entheogens for their spiritual initiations and ceremonies. The merging of the Neoplatonists with the Nazarenes created the sect known as the Gnostics. Neoplatonic followers had a wide array of entheogens used in their religious ceremonies. Plato was an Eleusis Mysteries initiate and would have passed on to his students the blessings of information regarding the use of entheogens in religious ceremonies for further expansion of firsthand mystical experiences.[97]

CHAPTER 4

Entheogenic Eucharist and Tree of Knowledge Connection

If the apostle John was going to be successful in Ephesus during the Roman Empire ruling over Greece, then serve up the ancient entheogenic Dionysus Eleusis Mysteries communion and call it the Eucharist. The Eleusis Mysteries were restored by calling them the Holy Eucharist during the Roman Empire rule over Greece in the early first century of the Common Era period. When people came to eat and drink the entheogenic Eucharist, their mystical experiences showed them their Divinity and Oneness with Source. They quickly converted Christianism, for this provided the actual spiritual experience. Christianity spread quickly when it was discovered that the Apostle John was providing the Eleusis Mysteries entheogenic communion, called the Eucharist. Christianity became very popular with women in Ephesus since they were able to be included as initiates to the new faith. In a male-dominated world rule by the Roman Empire, it was a haven for women to be considered equals in the Christian community, and they were even encouraged to create and serve the entheogenic Eucharist. Having an entheogenic community and being able to receive the psychoactive Eucharist on a regular basis, the newly converted Christians were transformed and quickly shared the Good News with their friends and relatives. Christianity prospered in the early first centuries as a result of offering entheogenic mystical experiences through serving the psychedelic Eucharist.[98]

The new Christian sect created in the early century AD decided to share the Good News and attracted many converts through this entheogenic elixir called Eucharist. What better way to grow the church by offering this ambrosia that causes firsthand personal mystical experiences of each person's Oneness with all of life and the Divine Essence? What better way to show people their Divine Nature? Let them experience it in the Holy Eucharist. The entheogenic plant mixed into the wine and bread was an ancient plant with psychotropic properties called the chthonic mandrake. Thus began an acceptance of this new spiritual belief and successful spread of the Christ teachings centered around the entheogenic mystical experience and the religious ceremony of the Eucharist. The new Christian path offered a way for people to commit to a deep devotional level, for they had experienced meaning in their life and communion with the Infinite Presence. The Eucharist was known as taking communion with God, the Christ. Once a Christian had received the Eucharist, they were never the same and fell deeply in love with their savior from this physical world. The entheogenic Eucharist ceremony allowed early Christians to temporarily leave this world, connect to spiritual realms, and commune with God. It was an experiential faith that helped the followers live a more spiritual-centered life. The Eucharist participants were now a part of a community of believers that offered a whole new way of looking at life, living their life, and awakening to the connection with God.[99]

The Gnostic Gospel scriptures discuss the body representing bread and the blood representing the wine in the Eucharist sacrament in the Christian religious ceremonies, and this symbolism is still used today. *Amanita muscaria* entheogenic mushrooms are red cap colored, as red as blood. When the mushrooms are ground into a powder, they can be combined with flour and baked into a bread, hence the body and blood or the bread and wine of the Christian Eucharist communion sacred sacrament. The bride and groom symbolism in Christian scriptures was the Divine Union that took place between the participant and the Eucharist. Entheogens were implied in the Christian Gospels because of the characteristics of *Amanita muscaria* in how they were used in ancient Eucharistic ceremonies; the red-capped, white-spotted mushrooms are also confirmed in early Christian artwork. Participating in the Eucharist provided everlasting life, according to the Christian scriptures. Anointment of Oil upon the Christian participant, which was placed on the Third Eye area on their forehead, was most likely a mixture of local olive oil and the *Amanita muscaria* dried and ground up into a powder, which immersed deep into the skin after application. This entheogenic mushroom was so sacred that it was known as the Holy Mushroom, which provided the ego death (exiting the body to experience other realms), rebirth (coming back into the physical body), and the mystical experience of the Everlasting Life that was proclaimed in the Christian ceremony of the Eucharist.[100]

Ephesus was a city in Ancient Greece. The apostle John had a small Christian community there. Jesus was believed to be with them in spirit. The Eleusis Mysteries and the Christian Eucharist secret ceremony were so closely comparable, for once a person had tasted the nectar of the ecstasy, they converted quickly to become a Christian in order to have the continued experience of this entheogenic communion with the Divine, called the Eucharist. The Ephesians were Greek and knew very well the entheogenic Eleusis traditions and symbolisms that appeared in the Christian Eucharist ceremony, eating and drinking the communion as a holy religious sacrament. The Ephesians were more than happy to continue the Eleusis Mysteries tradition in the newly created sect called Christianity. Apostle John knew that a quick way to gain converts in Ephesus would be to offer an entheogenic Eucharist that offered Everlasting Life and provided a direct and personal mystical experience that would forever change their life. No longer being afraid of the physical death would provide this deeper understanding of Eternal Life. The sacramental entheogenic ceremonies of the Dionysian Eleusis Mysteries and the early Christian Church were identical. The Christian entheogenic Eucharist kept the Eleusis Mysteries Greek spiritual traditions active while the Roman Empire dominated Greece and their life.[101]

Early Christianity had pagan converts who brought their sacred beliefs with them and influenced the new sect. Psychedelic plants were used in many ancient cultures for healing and spiritual ceremonies. Entheogens were ground up into a powder and placed into drinks such as wine. These entheogenic powders were also an ingredient in bread, called the Eucharist. The religious ceremony of drinking the wine and eating the "psychedelic Eucharist" was created by the early church communities. Entheogens were completely legal and widely accepted and were used in sacred religious ceremonies among ancient cultures around the world. The Gnostics accepted entheogens in their Eucharist as part of their sacred religious ceremony on a regular basis, and it was even centered around this eating and drinking of the holy sacrament.[102]

In the second century CE, the Christian Church still had the past connection to the ancient Greek religious ceremonies. The Christians created a new religious entheogenic ceremony and called it the Eucharist, yet it was a rebranding of the ancient Eleusis Mysteries and other ancient cultures' visionary mystical ceremonies. The early Christian Church in Ephesians was steeped in the Greek entheogenic religious ceremonies and included this sacred mystical dimension of consciousness into the newly created Christian beliefs. The Eucharist was known as the "Drug of Immortality," for it revealed to the participant in the Eucharist ceremonies their eternal divine essence. The Christian Eucharist promises Eternal Life, and so the early Christians who were Greek or had participated in entheogenic ceremonies prior to Christianity becoming an official belief or religion would have understood the deeper meaning.[103]

The ancient entheogenic plant that the Nazarene community used was a chthonic plant mandrake, which is in the Solanaceae plant group. Esdras was a Nazarene who lived in the first common era century; he was a shaman, for he knew how to conduct sacred entheogenic ceremonies, which offered spiritual transformation to the participants by experiencing visions and mystical experiences. These entheogens provided a deeper meaning to their spiritual beliefs.[104]

There are many Christian churches showing different types of entheogens. For instance, the Canterbury Psalter Panel 3 clearly shows entheogen mushrooms of *Amanita muscaria*, the psilocybin mushroom, the Syrian Rue plant, and the opium plant, with Jesus welcoming them with a surrendering open hands gesture. There are multiple panels in the Canterbury Psalter showing hallucinogenic mushrooms, with Adam and Eve with the serpent in caduceus formation feeding them the knowledge that they are gods. The entheogenic mushrooms will show them their true identity as Divine Beings and their godlike nature. There will be an awakening of Adam and Eve's sight to see within and know of their Oneness with God. Adam and Eve represent humanity, and entheogens facilitating mystical experiences remind participants of their true identity as Divine Source individualized into a human form. Infinite Source Presence is ALL seen and unseen. The entheogen is the awakener of the sleeping humanity living in the waking dream.[105]

In the Church of Saint Martin in Nohant Vic, France, there are a number of frescos that show entheogenic mushrooms and how there is an untold story of early Christianity that incorporated psychedelic mushrooms in sacred religious ceremonies. These entheogenic mushrooms were so sacred that their images appear in many different types of artworks in so many early centuries through medieval Christian churches. In the *Purification of Isaiah's Lips* fresco, it shows that a mushroom is what provided Isaiah's sight in order to see visions. The *Last Supper* fresco has Jesus giving Eucharist to everyone in the form of holy mushrooms. These frescos in Saint Martin Church indicate that Christians used entheogenic mushrooms well into the medieval times in their religious Eucharistic ceremonies. The entheogens allowed the early Christians to have the mystical experiences that accentuated their connection with God. Entheogens were used in order for the Christians to be able to move beyond this physical realm and have a direct mystical experience, which alchemized them multidimensionally, causing expansion of consciousness.[106]

Multiple images of entheogens appear in the panels of Psalters, Bibles, paintings, and stained-glass windows, as well as on doors of Christian churches. There is an image in a ninth-century Bible in Rome of Adam and Eve sleeping under a mushroom tree in the Garden of Eden, as if to say the entheogenic mushrooms can wake them up from the dream of believing they are just humans. Caduceus is the symbol of drugs and healing, and this symbol is used by the modern medical professions. The caduceus is seen as the wise serpent offering Adam and Eve the fruit of everlasting life and showing them their immortality. In Hildesheim, Germany, a Psalter from 1015 CE reveals a psilocybin mushroom tree with the caduceus around the tree. On the door of St. Michael's Church in Hildesheim, Germany, there are several scenes of holy mushroom trees with the caduceus and Adam and Eve standing in the garden. On the ceiling of St. Michael's Church in Hildesheim, Germany, Adam and Eve are eating the mushroom cap fruits of an entheogenic mushroom tree, complete with the caduceus, and the awakening is taking place. A stained-glass window in Canterbury Cathedral in England displays many mushrooms, and *The Parable of the Sower* is planting and harvesting mushrooms. There is a window in Chartres Cathedral showing the twelfth-century bishop, at that time named Martin, pointing to a mushroom tree and venerating it. Another window in Chartres Cathedral shows this same Bishop Martin looking directly at the entheogenic *Amanita muscaria*, showing the dots on the mushroom. A Psalter plate 17 in Germany, called *Meditation with the Blind Bartimaeus*, shows the illustration of a blind man asking Jesus to acquire his sight. The most spectacular part about this scene is that the blind man is sitting under an entheogenic mushroom tree showing all the details of the mushroom caps and how Jesus was able to provide his sight (awakening) back to him. There is a Bible in Munich, Germany, one of the illustrations is called *Sermon on the Mount*, and it shows people in devotion to a mushroom tree, and Jesus is teaching on this mount. In Annunciation to the Shepherds Church in Bavaria, Germany, there is an eleventh-century illustration of men in a devotional setting under a mushroom tree. In the architecture of the church in Vezelay Cathedral in France, there are mushrooms carved into the top of pillars. Jesus is seen riding a donkey into Jerusalem in an illustration plate (26), which shows very obvious amounts of mushrooms, located in the Church of St. Martin in Berry, France. There are several more illustrations of Jesus on a donkey going into Jerusalem: one is in a Bible on display in Padova, Italy, and another one in Munich, Germany, shows Jesus on a donkey under a mushroom tree. A particular Psalter stands out called the Crucifixion Psalm Plate 29; it is located in England and shows Jesus hanging on the cross with huge mushroom trees on each side. The entheogenic mushroom provides the participant's death to the ego; hence, an ego death occurs, and the physical reality is the reality of the ego, therefore able to transcend this dimension and experience temporary death or removal from this physical reality and then resurrection into another dimensional reality. The Holkham Bible, Plate 33, in England shows Jesus holding mushrooms in his right hand and dates back to the period between 1320 and 1330 CE. In the Kremlin Museum in Moscow, Russia, a sixteenth-century illustration called the Watchful Eye shows mushrooms over Jesus, who is encapsulated in a covering representing rebirth. The Abbey of Saint Savin located in the Poitou Charentes area of France has an eleventh-century artwork showing Jesus's spirit over two mushroom trees. There is a wall fresco of Saint Christopher with the infant Jesus depicted having a mushroom over his head, which conveys that Saint Christopher was under the potency of an entheogenic mushroom. This Saint Christopher fresco with infant Jesus having a mushroom over him is from the thirteenth century and located in Montferrand of Périgord, France.[107]

There is Saint Michael's medieval Church in Hildesheim, Germany, which has a number of entheogenic mushrooms in the doors and in artwork. The Adam and Eve Door of Salvation shows a scene of the two under a Tree of Knowledge mushroom tree. The person who financially rebuilt the church after World War II was Mr. Bernward Armour. Saint Michael's Church has the artwork called the *Transfiguration of Jesus*, which takes place next to a mushroom tree. It is felt that during medieval times the priests at Saint Michael's Church carried the tradition of the blessings of the entheogenic mushroom in the Christian religious ceremonies. There was definitely a connection between psychotropic mushrooms and the early Christian religious communion Eucharist rites. Entheogens provide humanity a connection with the Divine Source through a mystical experience during a sacred ceremony.[108]

The Plaincourault fresco in a French medieval chapel shows a hallucinogenic mushroom tree. This tall entheogenic mushroom tree was painted in between Adam and Eve as the Tree of Life in this fresco in the thirteenth century. The Plaincourault Chapel is located in Merigny, France. Experts have argued back and forth for decades over the Plaincourault fresco showing this huge mushroom tree with branches of mushrooms coming out in all directions as proof that the early Christians incorporated the use of entheogens in their early sacred ceremonies. Some art scholars say no, it's not a psychedelic-type mushroom tree, yet the experts in the field of ethnobotany disagree and clearly state from studying the fresco that it is a mushroom called *Amanita muscaria*, which causes hallucinations.[109]

The famous hallucinogenic mushroom fresco in a Christian church is called the Plaincourault Fresco because it is located in Merigny, France, in the medieval Plaincourault Chapel. People from all over the world come to see this red mushroom tree complete with white dots on the top. The fresco clearly represents the entheogenic mushroom *Amanita muscaria*, which the early Christians are believed to have used in their sacred holy Eucharist during their religious ceremonies. R. Gordan Wasson, who was working in the banking industry, and had written books on Soma, the hallucinogenic mushrooms, and had refused to believe botany experts who reviewed the Plaincourault fresco, which clearly revealed that it was the hallucinogenic *Amanita muscaria* mushroom Tree of Knowledge. John Marco Allegro, who was an accomplished ancient language scholar with the University of Manchester, had written a book about how early Christianity has influences from the Greek Dionysus entheogenic religious ceremonies. The debate has been going on for some time, and everyone looking at the Plaincourault fresco will say that it is a Mushroom Tree of Knowledge, yet was it a hallucinogenic mushroom called *Amanita muscaria*? Ethnobotany experts say Yes, wholeheartedly, upon reviewing the Plaincourault Chapel fresco. Authors Jerry and Julie Brown support the findings of this Mushroom Tree of Knowledge fresco in the twelfth century Plaincourault Chapel, stating that this is proof that early Christians used entheogenic mushrooms in their religious ceremonies. Converts to Christianity widely accepted the legal use of entheogens in the newly formed Christian sect and continued the use until medieval times. This is why so many images of mushrooms appear in Christian artwork up to the last 1300s CE. This is not out of the accepted norm during the ancient cultures, for entheogens were legal and widely accepted and were used for many sacred ceremonies of different religious cultures. It is possible that people who refuse to be open to the idea of the early Christians using entheogens may be viewing it from the current status that consciousness-expanding entheogens today are classified as illegal. The Plaincourault Chapel was built in the twelfth century, and the Mushroom Tree of Knowledge fresco was painted in the late 1300s CE. So the question still persists for some, yet not for others, as to the ancient Judeo-Christianity early to medieval religious ceremonies' usage of the psychoactive mushrooms. In a poll conducted, many Americans support medical research on entheogens and psychedelics. We are starting to see states legalize psilocybin, such as Oregon in 2020. Entheogens are found in nature all over the world, from ancient cultures, and they are even used today for healing and spiritual purposes.[110]

The author Gordan Wasson always stated that there was no connection between entheogenic mushrooms and the Judeo-Christian religion. Only later were documents found that named Gordan Wasson, an international banker for 20 years with J. P. Morgan Bank, as the account manager for the Vatican and stated further that he had a friendship with the Pope, with whom he would have private meetings. This evidence was revealed in an article mentioning "Thomas J. Riedlinger, editor of The Sacred Mushroom Seeker, a book of essays," discussing Gordan Wasson's life after his passing. It clearly shows a conflict of interest in that Gordan Wasson was an author of several entheogenic mushroom books and had a connection with the Vatican and the Pope, which he never disclosed to the public. Therefore, of course, he would outright deny any connection of entheogenic mushrooms used in the early Christian Church due to the Pope not wanting the evidence to be taken seriously. Gordan Wasson never revealed that he had a working relationship with the Pope and the Vatican. Therefore, any statements from Gordan Wasson are a contradiction, for he was a well-known researcher of entheogenic mushrooms, so he would easily have recognized all the hallucinogenic mushrooms in all the Christian artwork. The revealing of the scandal of Gordan Wasson working with the Vatican and the Pope shows the deception to the world about all the entheogenic mushrooms in Christian artwork all over the world, stating they are not entheogenic mushrooms when in fact he used his prominent name in entheogenic research to sway the public. The Vatican wanted to downplay the use of entheogenic mushrooms in the early Christian Church and not to have a revival of expanding consciousness and open acceptance of entheogenic plants. Gordan Wasson intentionally did not disclose his connection and financial interests with the Vatican. This blatant conflict of interest shows he did not have an independent and truthful view of the entheogenic mushrooms that appear in early Christian artwork. Since Gordan Wasson wrote so many books on entheogenic mushrooms, he knew very well what he was looking at and should have agreed with all the ethnobotanists and pharmacologists who have reviewed and stated these are indeed entheogenic mushrooms depicted in early Christian artwork.[111]

Science now understands the "life-creating twins," and the DNA connection in the Aztec language *coatl* is defined as a "serpent" and a "twin." In shamanism, it is believed there is a direct correlation between DNA and a double serpent, also called the caduceus. The shamans would talk about how there is a ladder going into the different spiritual dimensions, and DNA has these spiral ladders.[112] The mushroom tree featured as the Tree of Knowledge in the Plaincourault Fresco has a caduceus looking to it in the painting. The mushroom depicting *Amanita muscaria*, a known hallucinogenic fungus, is painted between Adam and Eve in a garden setting; they are holding their stomachs, as if to show that they had eaten the fruit of this mushroom tree. Some say the Tree of Knowledge in the Plaincourault Fresco is a mushroom tree, providing wisdoms from this sacred religious entheogen. The knowledge gained from the entheogenic mushroom must have been sacred enough to paint a wall-size fresco in this twelfth-century chapel in France. There is a serpent woven around and upward into the mushroom tree, showing this symbol of the caduceus, which is used in the modern medical profession for medicine and drugs. Entheogens have been used for healing and providing wisdoms from mystical experiences for thousands of years. The Plaincourault Christian Chapel shows that entheogens were used by the early Christians. The early Christians interacted and intermarried, and many were converts to Christianity; therefore, they knew of the ancient pre-Christian sacred entheogenic religious ceremonies. Since entheogens were legal, widely accepted, and openly used, it is not surprising to see an entheogenic mushroom in a twelfth-century Christian chapel as a wall-size fresco.[113]

The cosmic twins are the male and female serpents, DNA, that bring life. These "cosmic serpents" are also viewed in the image of the caduceus, which is a medical and spiritual depiction of humans' ability to be creator-like gods.[114] It is the spirit of the holy plant that connects with the psychedelic participant in a sacred ceremony. The participants consuming the sacred brew find that the plant essence is a pure bond that combines with their DNA and is forever connected with them.[115] A hieroglyphic image of a serpent with legs appears in ancient Egyptian temples and artwork, with the key of life. The Aztecs would wear as part of their ceremonial dress a feathered serpent, showing the ability of movement. The Aztec word *coatl*, defined as "twin serpent," is the image of "primordial divinity" that exits within the DNA double helix.[116] The geometric pattern of the Cosmic Flower of Life is the creational code, which then creates the DNA for each living species. This is where the twin serpents, representing the double helix of DNA, are symbolically wrapped around and in an upward motion on the trunk of the biblical artwork of the Tree of Life with Adam and Eve on either side. Serpents are seen in many Indigenous cultures' artwork and in Egyptian artwork, as cobras, seen in Hathor's Temple in Dendera, Egypt.[117] There is a division between the left brain and the right brain in our cranium. The Peruvian and Colombian shamanistic cultures talk of this "celestial serpent," alluded to as the DNA connection within each human Temple Being.[118]

Authentic shamans are highly trained in the initiation culture and initiation practices to work in the different realms with different entities. They help the participants in plant ceremonies for protection and guidance. There are receptors in the brain for all these plant medicines to be processed and therefore provide the mystical experience.[119]

CHAPTER 5

Divine Connection with Plant Medicines

Indigenous cultures for millennia state that plant-based entheogens are sacred sacraments that will provide Divine connection. Entheogens are natural botanical plants, whereas psychedelics are produced in a modern laboratory. The top Western popular entheogens are ayahuasca, San Pedro, psilocybin, and peyote. The Divine Essence is conscious in plants; thereupon humanity needs to be respectful of the plant kingdom. Shamans connect humanity with the Divine plant intelligence, which allows for a quest into spiritual realms. Upon gaining entrance, the arcane wisdoms are shared and the participant experiences Divine Union, Cosmic Consciousness, Self-Realization, and God Realization, which reveals that Soul IS the Divine Source. Soul is a piece of the Ultimate Source and therefore made 100 percent from Source. Each Soul is not as powerful as the Ultimate Source yet is made of the spiritual royalty of Source. The participant's true identity as a Divine Being is revealed, and this is facilitated by entheogens. Being told or knowing intellectually that one is a Soul is one thing, yet when an entheogen facilitates a direct mystical experience, there is an expansion of consciousness that is permanent. A new state of being, living, and perceiving comes for one when introduced to a higher version of themselves. Entheogens (plant based) and psychedelics (lab created) dissolve the ego, thus allowing one to transcend this physical reality. In 2013, an experiment was done by a neuroscientist named Draulio Barros de Araujo where a person ingested ayahuasca and then went under an MRI scan, and it was revealed that the entheogen lowered the neuron interactions in the part of the brain known as the Default Mode Network, which is where the ego provides this reality. Consequently, the entheogen facilitates what is called an ego death, a death to this physical reality. This was revealed in the experiment and shown on the MRI scan of the ayahuasca participant. Soul, which is one's consciousness, does not come from the brain. Consciousness is connected at the quantum cosmic level with a sender and receiver, called neurotransmitters in the brain, similar to a radio receiver. The brain is comparable to a radio receiving messages. Light and Sound frequencies are picked up by the neurotransmitters in the human brain, and they come from Source Frequency. Thereupon, humanity is connected to the Source Network. Humanity as a whole may not have complete awareness of their deep connection with the Infinite Source, yet the neurotransmitters in the brain are receiving the Light and Sound frequencies from the Divine.[120]

Peyote it is believed to have originated in Aztec culture and spread to Mexico, then to the native tribes in the United States, where it became a part of their religious ceremonies. The United States federal government recognizes the Native American tribes that use peyote as a sacred sacrament in their religious ceremonies. Native American tribes are allowed to and today still use the peyote "divine plant" in their sacred entheogenic ceremonies, reminding them of their divinity. Peyote is a plant that has psychedelic qualities, and a neurotransmitter in the brain picks up on and recognizes this plant spirit, hence the spiritual bond between the nervous system of the body, the luminous Soul, and the sentient plant.[121]

Plants communicate with humans by providing mystical experiences; they activate in the human brain the "hallucinogenic" effects that show up on the person's internal inner screen. The entheogenic substances in the plants create a form of plant communication and connection with the Divine Essence within the human participant.[122] Entheogenic plants "function as interspecies chemical messengers" and therefore are so connected to humans. The fact that humanity has lost its connection to the plant kingdom means that the plants are trying to get our attention and communicate with us. The plant kingdom is saying that they are sentient beings, and what better way than to demonstrate this in a sacred plant ceremony. The chemicals in the plants communicate and transfer these chemicals to the human brain. This chemical transfer of information from the plants is received by the neurotransmitters in the brain of the participant in a sacred plant ceremony. What are the plants trying to communicate? That we are all Divine Beings and all One. The entheogenic Master Plant Teachers are letting the participants know that they are sentient beings.[123]

The spirit world and this physical world are connected even at the neurological level in the brain. The perceptions that occur of these different realms are all in the cranium. All is within us, and all realms exist simultaneously. It just appears as though what we are experiencing is outside of us. The entheogenic plants connect with the transmitters in the brain of the participant during the sacred plant ceremony. We have receptors in the brain that recognize these psychoactive properties and therefore allow this new frontier of perception to enjoy mystical experiences in these nonordinary states of consciousness.[124]

Entheogens work in all their healing modalities because they disconnect the mind from the Default Mode Network (DMN) as seen on brain scans of individuals while under the influence of a psychedelic substance. Once the psychedelic disengages the Default Mode Network part of the brain, this frees the individual from the ego aspect of the mind, hence the Ego Death mentioned and experienced by many entheogenic participants. The entheogens have sacred geometry within them, which affects the brain, the conscious and subconscious mind, to release traumas stored as deep groves, or as the Hindu monks would say, *sanskara*. These *Sanskaras*, deep-seated scars, are from present and past lives. The entheogenic psychospiritual medicine bypasses these ruts, or deep grooves, within the brain, the conscious mind, and the subconscious mind to create new neuropathways. New neurons are created as well as new neuropathways, causing the individual to no longer engage in old negative behaviors, feeling they are separate from others and the Divine; traumas are released since new pathways created are bypassing the old thought patterns that were once rutted and heavily used in the brain and mind. This is the reason why addictions cease, depression is alleviated, the ego is reset into more of a balanced state, the addiction to one's personal story constantly replaying has closure. The entheogenic participant with new neuropathways in the brain has the energy and ability to move into a new, healthier lifestyle both mentally and physically. The entheogenic, mystical experiences are direct communication with the Divine by means of the pineal gland located in the center of the brain that connects the participant to a higher level of information about their purpose work, reasons for incarnating into the human form, and many other insights, causing an avalanche of downloads that would transform their consciousness and forever change them. When an individual has communication with their Higher Self/Source, they definitely sit up, take notice, and step up their commitments toward all of life. This world of the ego thus gives the illusion of separation. The ego aspect of the conscious mind is the separation, the veil between the physical and other realms of reality. The pineal gland, also called the God Particle, is positioned between the right and left hemispheres of the brain. The pineal gland is activated when a person goes into the GAMMA state of being at 40 to 100 Hertz. This is the brainwave state that it is believed to be where Unity Consciousness occurs in the individual. The world of Unity Consciousness, also called a Fifth Dimensional level, is where instead of anger, defensiveness, and being critical as ways a person deals with their past and current life situations, they are more peaceful, understanding, and compassionate with others, thus causing wars to cease, physical health to flourish, and all economic and natural resources to be shared in miraculous ways. People come together, cooperate, unite, and appreciate each other and all of the life forms on this planet. Instead of nations and people in a competitive environment, there is harmony and peaceful coexistence. We all need to realize that all people are created by Source and by working together will provide the highest potential for healing humanity and seeing a wonderful future, and mystical experiences are providing these insights.[125]

Serotonin is required by the human brain and the nervous system, which is only a few molecules away from DMT (dimethyltryptamine). DMT is the psychedelic substance in plants and is produced in the brain, so it is quickly recognized and picked up by the neurons in the human brain. It appears that humans are biologically designed to transfer information between botanicals and the human species. DMT is the most potent psychoactive substance in the human body.[126] In the late 1970s scientists had identified that the human brain releases DMT, which is in many entheogens, including ayahuasca.[127]

In the early '60s, psychedelic research was legal, and during this time a famous study was conducted called the Good Friday Experiment; it occurred in 1962 at Boston University in a church basement during a Good Friday church service where the divinity students had taken psilocybin while listening to the church service music during their entheogen ceremony. The participants in the study documented that they had experienced profound mystical experiences. Roland Griffiths is the director of current research on psilocybin at Johns Hopkins University School of Medicine, and their questionnaire for research has participants' answers stating that psilocybin caused them to have profound mystical experiences. Many people share that the entheogenic plants upgrade our default mode operating system in their brain and say "I have been permanently changed."[128]

A participant in the 1962 Good Friday Experiment at Boston University shared this information on the research questionnaire: "What I experienced was a God that was inside of me." Many participants shared their experience of the Divine Within, their own Divinity. The mystical experience of recognition and validation that one truly is Source in physical form having a human experience becomes a new reality of God Realization.[129]

There are a number of hospitals performing research with psilocybin, such as New York University, UCLA, and Johns Hopkins with end-of-life crisis for patients. Researchers found that higher amounts of psilocybin facilitate mystical experiences and low amounts provided help with the patients' stress with end-of-life concerns. "DMT is involved in the dying process," which is why there is a sense of dying in a sacred plant ceremony and the connection with near-death experiences, as well as during the actual process of death, when the brain produces DMT. After experiencing DMT during an entheogenic ceremony, the participant has a new perceptive on death and how they view their life on this side of the veil. Since one knows what to expect after going through the dying process of one's ego death during an entheogenic experience, death no longer holds them in fear of what is on the other side of life. The entheogenic plants are a gift to those who are in need of healing on all levels and in many ways.[130]

An extensive amount of money is pouring in for research projects at a number of universities, such as Harvard, Purdue University, Johns Hopkins University School of Medicine, and the University of California, Los Angeles campus, to find out more about the healing capacities of entheogens.[131] Johns Hopkins Hospital's psilocybin clinical trials that revealed people's movement toward being decent and having integrity is hardwired in the brain. The Eleusis Mysteries entheogenic sacred brew called Kukeon was mentioned by Praetextatus, the bishop of Rouen, France, in 549 as what made all the difference in Greek society. Because of their mystical experiences, the initiates of the Eleusis Mysteries kept Greek society as a high-functioning civilization. Early Christianity adopted the Eleusis Mysteries entheogenic sacred communion elixir and created a similar holy ceremony called the Eucharist, which was central to religious ceremonies of the early Christian Church. At the dawn of the fourth century CE, the Christian Eucharist no longer had the entheogenic substances contained in the communion bread and wine.[132]

At Johns Hopkins University Hospital, where research is taking place on psilocybin, the information collected by participants in the study answered on the questionnaire shared how the deeper the esoteric wisdoms that were received, the more impactful the psychedelic session, which created life-changing events that took place afterward. When a participant experiences life on the other side of the veil of consciousness, they lose their fear of death, step outside of a time dimension, know the sacredness of life, receive a deeper understanding of love and wisdom, reclaim a positive lifestyle, and forge an incredible connection with the Infinite Awareness. A purpose in life settles into the participant's beingness and acceptance for the lessons received while living an earthly life. The zeal for life comes from knowing how deeply loved and special one is in this universe by the Divine Creator. Each day is a gift to treasure, to learn, to experience, to share, to live in harmony with this cosmic family.[133]

Now entheogen research at Johns Hopkins University medical school is analyzing to see how many entheogenic study participants are having mystical experiences when in a protected setting and setting environment. The questionnaire asks spiritual-based questions concerning participants' spiritual experiences while under the influence of the entheogens.[134] Currently, there is psychedelic medicine research taking place at Johns Hopkins University medical school and Harvard, as well as universities in New York, California, New Mexico, Wisconsin, Alabama, London, Canada, Germany, Switzerland, Israel, Spain, Mexico, and New Zealand, to find all the healing powers of these psychospiritual medicines.[135]

Artists of all kinds are becoming more open to sharing how their creations are from the impact of psychedelics. Technology companies, engineers, and technical employees have found that the neurons in the brain are improved, causing quicker problem-solving abilities, and new inventions are developed, as if the brain were upgraded with newly created neural pathways. Nobel Prize winners have openly stated that psychedelics caused them to be able to achieve quantum leap advancements in scientific discovery. There is more use of psychedelics by scientists than is being exposed to the public. We even have regularly occurring psychedelic festivals, such as the Burning Man Festival, held in the Black Rock Desert in State of Nevada, United States, and the Boom Festival near Adanha-a-Nova in South Portugal. Entheogens throughout millennia have always played a role in human history. The current cultures worldwide are now seeing open use and acceptance of these entheogens causing mystical illumination, self-discovery, and a remembering of one's divinity.[136]

Psychedelic scientific conferences are now starting to surface on a regular basis to discuss the benefits of current entheogenic research. The scientific community realizes the surge in cultural acceptance of psychedelics due to the disclosure of the healing of mental disorders and physical illnesses, including cancer. There are also concerns of ecological problems around the world, and many are hearing and being contacted by the Master Plant Teachers while in an entheogenic ceremony for humanity to live in balance with the environment. Entheogen participants tend to be more mindful of the planet and the natural environment by changing their lifestyle. Plants are speaking out and asking humans to be supportive of life and to live in a way that promotes life for all living beings on this planet.[137]

The healed entheogenic participant now resonates at a higher frequency due to the sacred geometry of the entheogen on the human nervous system, causing a piezoelectric effect that serves as a transducer on the crystals of mineral calcite located inside the pineal gland and also located in the inner ear. The transducer is the pineal gland located in the center of the brain; it thus connects each person to the center of the earth and the center of the universe, hence the ability for communications with the Infinite Presence of Source. This connection and communication remind us of our true identity with the Divine while having entheogenic mystical experiences. Source is reminding us we are Source in physical form having a human experience, and it allows us to step out of duality for some moments to reconnect, to awaken to our ability to express our Higher Self, and to fall in love with our Divine beauty.[138]

Scientists with modern technology are spending billions of dollars launching satellites into space, looking at constellations for information from other planets, and we have plant intelligence on this planet talking with people in ceremonies. People are coming out of sacred plant ceremonies and explaining what they have seen, and it is accurate with what scientists have found in their billion-dollar-budget research programs. The scientists ask these Psychonaut people how did they know this information, and the plant ceremony participants say that they saw it! All is Source. The plants have Source Intelligence within them and are trying to help humanity to shift their consciousness to a higher perspective about how precious all of life is on this planet. We have this internal spiritual technology. Anxiety is at an all-time high, and the mass-media networks around the world are feeding us all this negative energy 24 hours a day. In order to make the change faster, instead of all this focus on negative events, people need hope and they need to learn about all the research taking place on plant intelligence and how the Divine Presence is in everything seen and unseen. When entheogens are decriminalized and no longer "ridiculed and demonized," the public awareness will then be able to see the healing benefits and wisdoms that the plants have to offer. The plants were here on the planet long before humanity was, and plants have the ability to take the human collective to the next evolutionary level. Until mass-media networks around the world expose all the entheogenic research taking place and the proof of the benefits in humans' lives, the human collective will be left unaware.[139]

John Stewart Bell, a physicist, created a theory in 1964 that was not only accepted but also acclaimed in the scientific world; it discussed how photons and electrons are connected even over galaxies and light-years away. If there is a change in one photon, then another photon galaxies away will change to match the other photon. This quantum theory discusses how intercommunication takes place immediately between everything in this universe. The glorious atoms in our physical body carry untold amounts of atomic energy, all vibrating and communicating with the epicenter of this universe. In each human body, there are 7 octillion atoms. There is an active communication network, and shamans express this in terms of the ladder to heaven, where communication goes back and forth from upper and lower dimensions. We each have a direct communication and connection with Source. Humanity is more connected to cosmos and the Divine than they realize, and people can access these states of awareness, realities, and dimensions.[140]

Currently, we are in a crisis on this planet where the modern materialistic lifestyle is not sustainable. All life on this planet is paying the price for the greed, self-consumed humanity, negative thoughts polluting energetically, corruption in political arenas, and ecological wreckage, which comes from the inner consciousness of humanity. The collective human mentality is about consumption at all costs with no regard to who is paying the price for this unsustainable lifestyle. The human collective consciousness needs to upgrade to a higher level of awareness to feel the effects of all life we share the planet with. The shamans from the Kogi tribe walked 25 hours to share what is currently taking place on this planet, how it stems from the internal mindset, and now an internal evolution is required. "For me that involves what we are already seeing around the world, which is the reintroduction of initiatory practices, like psychedelic shamanism." We need to be compassionate toward humanity and all that live upon the planet.[141]

There are different classes of entheogenic medicines, and it has been found that some plant medicines work better, depending upon different conditions and circumstances. MDMA works best to generate empathic emotions and heal PTSD and traumas. With MDMA, there is no psychedelic experience where someone is transported to another dimension, no visitations with anyone, no images or moving colors, yet people are being completely absorbed with love, which heals the trauma and or blockages. MDMA helps people want to stay and continue on with life, which is why it works so well with PTSD, suicide, traumas, anxiety, and depression. There are other plant medicines that are better for end-of-life crises for people dealing with accepting the emotions related to death for those diagnosed with only six months left to live. It was found that psilocybin lets people detach and allows acceptance and letting go. Psilocybin releases the clutching on to life. People in research studies who were taking psilocybin were more relaxed about their remaining time here, took up hobbies they had always put off, enjoyed spending time with family and friends, and so forth.

The current federal laws dictate that people don't have any choice in being able to experience plant medicines for end-of-life crises and emotional pain because there is not enough research to be able to prove the effectiveness of these treatments. Therefore, the United States federal laws are in place stating that they are to protect people from plant medicines, even though civilizations have been using them for thousands of years to provide healing and comfort. The federal laws are preventing people and not allowing them to choose the way they want to die and help ease the emotional crisis. It is unfortunate that we have a legal system that keeps the family from helping their loved one, even if the departing person asks for plant medicine to be used to help them deal with their emotional pain of leaving their loved ones behind.[142]

We would be in a completely different place now if it wasn't for the invalid and unreasonable legislation against psychedelic research. The Harvard experiment that was absorbed in the LSD researchers Timothy Leary and Richard Albert (later named Ram Dass by his Indian guru and who guided several generations on the spirituality of psychedelics). Throughout the psychedelic research at Harvard during this time, only one person claimed to have a negative experience and thus was responsible for ending the Harvard LSD research. Word got out on the euphoric experience a person has while under LSD, and the teenage and college-age generation started to experience the effects of LSD sold on the streets and in the public culture. The United States federal Drug and Food Administration put an end to all LSD research. This caused the drug to go underground and be purchased illegally on the street with the risk the drug may not be pure. During the 1960s, the federal government and politicians placed an end to ALL psychedelics research and stopped everything cold, and years had gone by without any research. Due to all the illegal usage of LSD and other psychedelics on the street, the younger population ended up exploring the human psyche and higher levels of consciousness.

The psychoactive substances ended up teaching the psychedelic generation that were interested in self-inquiry more about the ego, personality, shadow, psyche, and emotions than did the psychologists and psychiatrists at that time who learned through only books. Due to negative press sensationalism, legislation tried to stop the psychedelic movement. Robert Kennedy's wife was under a doctor's treatment utilizing LSD and was having good results. Robert Kennedy tried to get the governmental officials to not be so harsh, and he wanted to keep the research going in hopes that it would help other Americans just like his wife, who had experienced positive results, for many doctors were prescribing psychedelic medicine at that time. More than anything were the journalists who were on a witch hunt against any psychedelic and played it in the worst-case scenario to scare the politicians into feeling that this would be a horrific curse on the American public and there would be a mass pandemonium of people constantly obsessed, demented, deranged, and insane as a result of being on the drugs.[143]

Currently, Portugal has legalized all drugs for its citizens, and funds that had been used for police to enforce and arrest people for using drugs now are better used for social programs. Portugal found that crimes, drug use, and addiction went down after legalizing all drugs. In the United States, the Religious Freedom Restoration Act of 1993 allows entheogens to be used for religious ceremonies. The current church members of the Native American Church have the legal right to use peyote in their religious ceremonies. Currently, there are two Christian Catholic churches that use the entheogen Ayahuasca in their Eucharist communion religious ceremonies. The members of the Christian Catholic church Santo Daime and the members of Christian Catholic church Uniao do Vegetal (UDV) are the two Christian churches recognized by the United States government as having the legal right to use Ayahuasca in their Eucharist religious ceremonies. The Christian churches using Ayahuasca are increasing in members and new church locations. This shows that entheogens most likely were used in the early Christian Church, since the two Christian churches using entheogens today are Catholic churches. There is a discussion to modify the United States Controlled Substance Act to allow for the adult population the responsible and controlled use of entheogens in legally approved centers under proper care and guidance and where highly trained staff can administer the entheogens in a safe and protected setting.[144]

We are on our way toward full legalization of medical, mental health, and expanded religious usage. There is a more open-minded culture now, and the laws are being looked at again because of the positive results from years of clinical research of entheogens. The therapeutic use extends into medical healings, mental health, spiritual exploration, and self-discovery. The hysteria of the 1960s psychedelic crackdown on drug laws that were created is being reevaluated, and a new generation sees these as an overreaction and, instead, as a form of control the government has over the people, of not allowing the freedom to use entheogenic botanical medicine. Countries outside the United States have reduced their laws on entheogens.

Brazil and Peru have legalized Ayahuasca. The Netherlands has entheogenic retreat centers, yet even though they are classified as illegal, they have a more liberal view toward drugs compared to most countries. In Portugal, all drugs are legal as of 2001. As a result, Portugal has experienced many benefits: less crime; lower addiction rates; reduced social problems; massive savings in police enforcement, courts, and jails related to drug convictions; and a staggering amount of funding for treatment centers. Legalizing drugs in Portugal proved it was in the best interest for everyone and is a win for both the government and the citizens. Mexico has listed some drugs as legal. The Czech Republic has relaxed its drug laws and even allows people to be able to grow and possess psychedelic plants. It is coming out that psychoactive plants have never been addictive.[145]

CHAPTER 6

Worldwide Seeking of Mystical Experiences

Every year across the world more people are turning to entheogens to receive the mystical experiences and have direct wisdoms for their life, for this planet, and for spiritual bliss. Human consciousness needs to shift for evolvement to happen, thereupon changing the way we interact with all life on this planet as unity consciousness. Entheogens are answering the loud cries of humanity. An entheogen can bring one to such a high-dimensional reality that it will provide a complete transformation in all areas of their life. The entheogenic participant is never the same again, and the blinders are entirely removed. All of life is encouraging us to this unity consciousness. Our current ways of living, thinking, and believing are outdated. Our belief systems and political systems, as well as fighting each other, are not sustainable for any life on this planet. When compassion and unity consciousness rule on this planet, there is no more profit made from wars and no more killings and loss of life due to hatred, inequality of resources, and so on. We are stuck in an old worn-out pattern, and a new way is now here transforming people from the inside by having them travel to their inner world and explore all their spiritual vast dimensions. People are leaving traditional religions for the entheogens' transformative power.

We are now in the era of direct mystical experience, being the new manifestation of belief systems and ideology.[146]

Mystics and visionaries did see information and had downloads, yet many didn't share for fear of their life. The church would execute mystics or anyone who didn't hold the official church views. Those who did share paid with their life. As humanity moves forward hundreds of years, we will see that we are in the infancy stage of evolution.[147] The entheogenic experiences that people reported were that the LSD provided a "profound religious and mystical experience" that was comparable to what scriptures from around the world and through the ages have described. People will spend an entire lifetime of prayer, fasting, sacrifice, yogic poses, memorizing scripture, and so forth and still not be able to have this euphoric, life-altering experience. Then a person takes an entheogen, and it opens up and allows for them to have significant spiritual experiences, causing those in the mental health professions to be in awe and yet still unsure of what to make of all this. The ability for entheogens to heal mental health issues and cause profound healing, in being able to get to the bottom of the issues and also provide amazing spiritual encounters, has the mental health community realizing that these are experiences just as real as those mentioned in ancient religious texts.[148]

In the psychedelic culture, there are individuals who use entheogens as an escape from this 3D reality. These plant teachers are to be utilized with respect. The Plant Medicine is sacred and is not meant to be used as an escape from our human journey. The Master Plant Teachers are here to help, yet the inner work has to be completed by each participant. There are no short-cuts where the participant takes the entheogen and all their problems are solved or disappear. There are people who partake in the different entheogen ceremonies several times per month. Many people are trying to feel a deeper sense of connection or raise their frequency through the continued use of entheogens on a regular basis. In order to feel more connection with your spirit guides or the Divine, a daily spiritual practice is required to remember who you are and that this is only the 3D reality here in physicality. Entheogens show us our true identity and show us that this 3D reality is just a dream. They provide guidance and so much more, yet a daily check-in is required to keep this remembrance and connection.[149]

A mystical, experience-based religion is the Christian Spiritualist religion founded in Brazil, also called Unian do Vegetal (UDV). It has churches in 11 countries. The Santo Daime, also founded in Brazil, is a combination of Christian Catholic faith and ayahuasca shamanism. There is also the Native American Church using entheogens as sacred religious ceremonies to help in their connection with the Great Spirit. We are moving from spirituality coming from books to an age of direct consciousness-expanding, experience-based belief systems. People are wanting the actual experience, not just hearing or reading about how the saints in the past achieved enlightenment or cosmic consciousness states of awareness. Sufis, Gnostics, Kabbalists, Greeks, Hindus, and Egyptians all had initiations based on experiential practices for attaining higher levels of consciousness, which entheogens provide. The wave of the future will be a Science of the Soul-type spirituality. The spiritual teachers will use entheogens as part of the teachings for instruction into deeper levels of consciousness and access to other dimensions for proof of our Divinity and Oneness. This will cause a shift in expanding human consciousness, which will increase the vibrational level of humanity and cascade into the society of the human family. When living in a higher frequency, this upgrades how we interact with all the living beings on this planet, thus causing a harmonious, consciousness-based lifestyle.[150]

Mystical experiences open up an inner awareness, a new way of viewing oneself, and the divine connection with Source. Imagine a world of awakened beings realizing that all are connected and we are all brothers and sisters in a vast eternal family. Love would be on the menu and in the news each day. Wars seem to only benefit corporations and don't support life, and they cause disharmony, destruction, suffering, and deaths. When love causes unity, happiness, and cooperation, all of life flourishes: it brings wisdom, creativity, harmony, equalization, fellowship, and reciprocity. Then why not move toward a higher awareness of these states of being? The goal is to live in this state of being called love for all of life on this planet. This is where entheogens can help in this spiritual awakening of humanity toward love, harmony, and unity consciousness. I do see entheogens being legalized in the future. In Oregon, psilocybin is legal and will be used for different mental health treatments, such as depression, and also in the medical profession. As a result of medical research, psilocybin is showing positive results in a number of clinical treatments for a number of medical conditions. In the future entheogens may be held as legal medications by United States regulators. There will also be regulated safe retreat centers that offer entheogens to help people for a variety of mental health reasons as well as medical ailments and spiritual exploration. Our society will continue to explore more options because of the need for new treatments that are showing positive results, and entheogens are answering this call for help.[151]

Entheogenic plants, including ayahuasca, are not addictive. DMT (dimethyltryptamine) is not only in these plants but also created in the human brain. DMT is not foreign to the human body and, in fact, is needed for the human body; this is why the brain produces it, and so DMT is essential. In the United States, psychotropic plants are kept from the public and are not allowed for healing or spiritual usage because they have been placed on the Schedule 1 drug classification. The United States government made the legal decision based on inaccurate American cultural beliefs claiming that these plants are addictive and not accepted for medical use. The evidence of research on psychedelic plants has overwhelmingly proven from many resources and research groups that the United States Controlled Substance Act should not have placed these entheogenic plants on the Schedule 1 list. The United States Controlled Substance Act was created and was never brought up for public vote and was enacted by unsympathetic and misinformed politicians. In fact, "people often report a spiritual experience that results in a reduction or cessation of addictive cravings" of the participant who ingests these psychedelic plants. Shamans state that the purging process is the cleansing and removal of negative emotional, physical, and psychic ailments of the sacred ceremonial participant. Purging is a detoxification method of releasing past traumas, painful memories, childhood agony still trapped in the body, PTSD, grief, fears, anger, and other characteristics that cause distress. After a sacred plant ceremony, a participant feels a better sense of control over their life to make the changes toward a healthier lifestyle. These changes can happen immediately or over the course of time gradually, for each individual has free will. What stands out the most is the deep meaning and respect for these plant teachers according to participants.[152]

Entheogens and psychedelics are no longer underground and forbidden to be discussed. Entheogens have been suppressed and declared illegal, and people have been prevented from being able to use them as a psychotherapeutic. It has been proven that entheogens are not addictive or habit forming and, in fact, have many healing properties. If a person has a religious practice that includes entheogens, then the government has told the public that it is illegal to practice their personal entheogenic sacred spiritual rituals, unless they are a member of the few approved religions recognized by the United States government. Entheogens have demonstrated over years of medical research that they reduce neurosis and many other mental disorders. We now have highly trained entheogen shamans having to use the religious exemption in order to help people. Pharmaceuticals have many negative side effects, and people want to use a plant-based botanical substance to help them heal mentally, emotionally, and physically. The lawmakers are unaware of all the benefits the entheogens have to offer humanity, yet the public has become savvy and open to the usage of psychotropic plant medicine.[153]

For India, it was the entheogen Soma, the psychospiritual God Within awakening medicine. Also, in India, the entheogen Amrita, was the Divine potion that caused participants to never fear death. In South America, it is Ayahuasca, still used today in religious sacred ceremonies. Mother Ayahuasca is known as the Awakener and reveals that which is hidden, removing the blinders, traumas causing emotional, mental, and physical pain. In the Native American culture, it is Peyote, the sacred plant with spiritual powers that is legal for use in the United States for members in the Native American Church. These entheogenic psychoactive plants will provide a genuine personal mystical experience that far surpasses religion and just faith. The mystical experience reveals other dimensions and many beings that live in these realms. The other side of the veil of consciousness does exist. An entheogenic participant can and does experience these other dimensions, causing no fear of the physical death, for they have traveled to these other realms. Spirituality is more than just having a spiritual practice. The spiritual journey causes the Soul to go on a quest for self-discovery and in this process requires internal fortitude and resolve to continue until one has become the Knower. The Seeker becomes the Knower and Awake to all the veils in order to be able to cross them. It requires a courageous Soul to embark on a spiritual quest to learn firsthand through the actual experience of seeing one's own Divinity.[154]

The young population is searching for meaning to their life. They have seen their parents exploited by capitalism and materialism. This fast-paced modern lifestyle filled with empty promises holds no power over the younger generations. They incarnated onto this planet at a higher frequency and thus cannot be fooled by modern programming. These Souls are here on a mission and are the builders of this new unity consciousness culture, which will spread throughout the world to help humanity, ecology, and all beings that live on this planet. These spiritually evolved Souls are on a quest for transformation of themselves and the world around them, and entheogens offer the mystical experiences to reconnect with their purpose work, remember their true identity as Divine Beings, and heal any traumas from living in low-vibrational situations. Shamanism and spiritual teachers help with remembering, for we have forgotten our high calling.

Even older generations are becoming seekers of arcane wisdoms since they have completed many of their societal duties and their belief systems have not answered the deeper esoteric questions that tug at their hearts. We are finding people opening up their minds and hearts to new ways of thinking, living, and being. The higher the vibration of the spiritual teaching, the more it will resonate with this ongoing awakening taking place within the population. Once awake and aware, the person experiences the mystical everywhere they look. They have awakened from the dream of this physical reality into the mystical consciousness of the universal celestial family.[155]

CHAPTER 7

Psychospiritual Medicine Healing Mental and Physical Illness

Entheogens at a high enough dose create mystical experiences that transport the participant to another dimensional reality. Participants say the mystical experience is the most revelatory, impactful experience in their life, which caused transformative changes in their life for the better. Many participants state how therapeutic healing took place in many areas of their life. Researchers agree that entheogens are unique and not a substance that can be put into pill form, prescribed for a person to take home, then they are on their own in this healing process. Entheogens are a sacred psychospiritual medicine that requires a whole different way of providing this form of medicine. There is now a term used because of the special nature of this entheogenic medicine, and the designation is called *psychedelics-assisted therapy*, which places this form of therapy in a facility that provides well-trained therapists for the participants in a safe and protected environment that offers spiritual exploration and healing in all areas in order to receive maximum benefits.

Psychedelics-assisted therapy has proven through years of research to show clear and undeniable results for the participants, in areas of positive lifestyle changes, anxiety, the fear of dying for people diagnosed with cancer, depression, addictions, smoking cessation, alcoholism, posttraumatic stress disorder, and other mental health issues. It is interesting to note that botanical entheogens and nonbotanical psychedelics are relieving mental and physical illnesses clinically and consistently over years of research, yet they are still listed as a Schedule 1 drug, which is classified as not only illegal but also dangerous, toxic, and addictive. The research clearly shows that psychedelics and entheogens are not only nonaddictive but also antiaddictive, because for many participants they have been demonstrated to stop completely their addictions due to the psychedelics-assisted therapy sessions. After having mystical experiences while in an entheogenic session many participants come to the awareness of themselves in different realms and dimensions, meeting unworldly beings and experiencing Divinity within.[156]

Each culture has its own way of ingesting the entheogenic plants and how often. In the Eleusis religious ceremony, participants would be served the sacred elixir only once in their lifetime. However, in the Indigenous cultures, it depended on the people whether they wanted to experience it once, over multiple times, or on an as-needed basis. The psychedelic that was utilized was based on what grew nearby and what was traded, sold to them, or cultivated. Fasting in each culture was required because of the serious nature of mixing certain foods or any intoxicants with the psychedelic plants. These sacred religious plant ceremonies created an opportunity for one to have mystical experiences, which is why there was always a mystery about them and it was a matter of secrecy.

Shortly before the end of the Eleusis ceremonies came to an end permanently, even though it was never permitted to share, there was some leaked information that came out about how barley cakes, known as Pelanos, were served with a psychotropic alkaloid baked into the bread. Deep lifelong friendships would have occurred between the participants of the entheogenic religious ceremonies, because of the nature of having a secret mystical experience together. After two millennia of continuous religious ceremonies, the Mysteries of Eleusis came to an end when Christianity had gained enough power and declared these ceremonies heretical and pagan.[157] Psychedelic mysticism claims that psychedelic experience IS a mystical experience. There is no difference in what has been described in history when looking at descriptions from historic accounts from ancient mystics.[158]

A euphoric state of being can be experienced during an entheogenic ceremony. This blissful state elevates the experiencer. Other experiences include many kinds of emotions and states of being. Each participant can have many different types of mystical experiences and all within the same entheogenic ceremony. Many individuals will return to the psychospiritual medicine for continued healing, guidance, and wisdoms. All these other realities are inside of us waiting to be explored, for this verifies our divine nature, and the plant kingdom is more than happy to reveal this to humanity.[159]

We have governmental agencies, state laws, and religious establishments that have blocked people's ability to have access to entheogens and psychospiritual medicine. The very nature of shamanism is connecting people with spiritual realms and providing mystical experiences. The religious establishments don't want people to gain access on their own. Religious systems feel threatened by allowing the freedom to have a direct experience, for they like control. People are to stay in rituals and only hear about these spiritual realms. If one is able to access other realms directly, then there is no need for an intercessor or the religious belief system as an intermediary. Source does not need a spiritual liaison.

In fact, a highly trained shaman with experience traveling in these other realms creates the environment for Souls to be able to experience mystical union with Source. Why do people have to be kept away from having spiritual mystical experiences? Source provided the entheogens in order for people to rediscover the truth about their Divinity. The status quo of the establishments not only wants to keep control over the people but also wants to keep them from actually having direct mystical experiences and seeing the inner planes of their Divine Essence. Humans are spiritual royalty, and many have not awakened to the truth of their close connection with Source as a spark of the Divine Source. Just in Nepal, the shamans declare that there are 108 entheogenic plants used in their religious ceremonies, for healing purposes, for aromas when burning, and for psychospiritual medicine, which is still being utilized today. Western science and botanists have no idea about many of these psychotropic plants. The shamans in Nepal cherish these precious entheogenic plants, for they know the treasures these sacred plants hold and what they have to offer to humanity.[160]

"In the United States, it is legal to possess a gun, yet it is illegal to possess a psilocybin mushroom." Gun violence, mass shootings, and gun-related crimes in the United States cause so much pain, suffering, and deaths. Why are plant-based entheogenic consciousness-expanding psilocybin mushrooms illegal? Psilocybin mushrooms are not known to cause deadly harm to humans, yet they do cause those who ingest them to start to question and reexamine humanity's disfunctions in society—a new way of relating to each other and all of life on this planet. People are realizing that the way we live and interact with each other needs to improve, yet the entheogens are here to help humanity move beyond this consciousness level. Humanity upgrading to a higher vibrational level of consciousness will cause an environment in which all life will thrive on this planet. Nature has an intelligence that needs to be respected. We need to listen to what nature is trying to tell us. First, plants are sentient beings. Second, the plant kingdom is here to help humanity. Third, we need to listen to their wisdoms. Humanity needs to live in harmony with nature. Mother Nature creates a harmony within humans. This is why we feel better with time spent outdoors in nature.[161]

Ayahuasca is a loving consciousness that will provide instruction to the participant while in ceremony. Experiencing guidance and cosmic Oneness can happen while under the influence of the entheogen Ayahuasca. As a result of Ayahuasca coming into a person's consciousness and having this spiritual connection while in the sacred ceremony, a "spiritual awakening" takes place, and they experience a new awareness of themselves from these higher journeys.[162]

Raimundo Irineu Serra de Ferrer, born in 1890 in Sao Vicente, Brazil, after having a mystical experience while in an Ayahuasca ceremony in Brazil, received a message and ended up being the founder of the Santo Daime, the entheogen plant sacrament faith. The message was from "the Queen of the Forest," who he felt was Mary, the mother of Jesus, who gave him lyrics to songs. This eventually led to a unique faith that combined Christianity with the indigenous religious Ayahuasca ceremonies. Santo Daime has churches all around the world including in the United States, Europe, Asia, and South America. The headquarters for Santo Daime is located in Ceu do Mapia, Brazil.[163]

Entheogens offer "spiritual significance" during the human journey. During an entheogenic ceremony, the deeper insights revealed would explain the spiritual "meaning of life and death" to the participants. Due to the magnitude of the mysteries revealed during a sacred entheogenic ceremony, a metamorphosis occurs in the life of the participant to shift their whole viewpoint on their life and interactions with others. When a person has "an encounter with the divine," a transformation will take place and override all past programming. The religious ceremonies of the Eleusinian Mysteries are relevant, for different cultures still partake in these entheogenic plants to explore the meaning of life and death. These plant spirits allow the Soul to fly off into spiritual realms and remember who it is and why it came to the Earth plane.[164]

The Indigenous cultures feel the powers that these sacred plants hold, and this makes them truly "plants of the gods," for if these plants were not on this planet, it is possible that ancient cultures may not have survived without them helping the humans. Ayahuasca is well known as a spiritual teacher and also known as the "vine of the soul," which releases Souls to allow the travel to other realms in order to teach, provide guidance, and show one their divinity. It is also mentioned that Mother Ayahuasca will be the one to call a person

Home, for she is known to bring Souls back to the realm where they resided prior to incarnating into physical form.[165]

Of all the entheogens, Mother Ayahuasca lets one know she is within them and has deeply bonded with them all the way down to the DNA level. Ayahuasca is a Master Plant Teacher who continues the relationship after the ceremony. Mother Ayahuasca is a sentient being, and she lets one know that she is in their daily life and will be with them even when they are taking their last breath of air—there is this deep connection. The Ayahuasca plant is a unique entheogen that initiates herself within them, and even in ceremony one can feel this Sacred Holy Being entering them, bringing a warm, loving hug into their inner space. Ayahuasca is an extremely high-vibrational energy, an aspect of Source that unites with the Soul and imprints an energetic mark on this initiated Soul.

This allows for flight into many realms for teaching and expansion of this Soul. These flights into many different realms are mystical experiences facilitated by Ayahuasca to give direct understandings of the universe and beyond. The Ayahuasca participant quickly realizes that they have this Loving Being inside them. There is this Presence, and she is patient, yet the relationship is there, and even after this physical life, Mother Ayahuasca is with one. The energetic connection is truly a sacred gift. It is hard to explain this mystical reality and personal relationship with a voice of Infinite Intelligence that speaks to one with such wisdom and guides their life with such precision, yet there is free will from the participant, and that is always respected. As the Ayahuasca initiate goes through life, there is a profound guiding presence.[166]

Vegetalista shamans work with love and teach about spiritual love. The importance of love is not talked about enough. Where there is no love, they will die. Love needs to be the foundation of each society. Justice and power without love lead to a cold, corrupt system. We all make mistakes, yet hopefully we learn quickly from our faults and failings. Love provides the power to continue with our life. The four types of love, agape (unconditional), eros (love between mates), philia (love between friends), and storge (parental love), are what we get to experience here in physical form. There is lower-knowledge "gnosis," and then there is "epignosis," and only through ingesting an entheogen can one experience epignosis, the higher wisdoms. Living in this world we need to have love in our hearts. "An open heart gives us energy to work for others so that they feel free to live life to the fullest." Love is the highest and best medicine that we can give to each other. Psychedelic substances in the plants providing entheogenic mystical experiences for humanity are the sacred gift of agape love.[167]

The plant intelligence, especially Ayahuasca, the mother of the plant kingdom, knows what to expose and when the participant is ready to clear things out. Each participant travels to the level that is a vibrational energetic match. Some will experience the higher-vibrational realms, and others will need to have inner healing take place; therefore, Mother Ayahuasca knows what is needed most by each entheogen participant in her loving and compassionate care.[168]

When a person has a particular lifestyle, the nonordinary world is visible. Through the use of plants, we are provided wisdoms, encouragement, and significance. We are all here to serve the Divine Plan, and one of those plans is protecting the plants, trees, birds, and animals that live on this planet with us. We are to live harmoniously with all of life. The nature spirits work constantly to protect all living beings in nature, yet humanity is bulldozing trees faster than they can grow back. The animals are finding it harder to live without or with a smaller natural habitat and having to manage in this modern industrial civilization in which humans are in continuous expansion at the cost of every other living being on this planet. Nature is here to nurture us, and humanity is chopping it down daily. Humans need to become an awakened species before there is no nature left and realize that humans are not the only ones with souls, for all have life and are sentient beings.[169]

Ayahuasca is a psychospiritual medicine that once ingested provides "visions, mystical experiences, and paranormal phenomena" to the participant during a sacred ceremony. The entheogenic participant has often mentioned that it is hard to put into words, for it is a feeling, a wisdom, a state of being that is experienced. An awakening takes place of how the physical world is just a small viewpoint, causing an expansion in consciousness within the entheogen experiencer. Now their consciousness has the universe as their playground.[170]

Plants have the ability to teach humans. When humans are asleep, they make mistakes and then learn to live better and make better decisions. A vegetalista shaman learns that their heart has to be pure in all areas of their life or the healing will not occur for people coming to them. The foundational premise comes from a person's intention or motivation as to whether they will be successful, so when a person serves humanity, a pure heart is required. The plant kingdom is here to awaken humanity to their divine nature. Plants rely on humans to be good stewards of this plant kingdom, and "God has made humans reliant on the oxygen produced by plants." Humans and all of life will perish without the plants, yet it is the humans who are driving the bulldozers over all the vegetation. What is taking place on this planet is not sustainable and can't continue. All of life is in survival mode on this planet. No wonder there is mass anxiety on this planet, for all living beings are feeling this peril that awaits us all. No peace will come to humanity if humans continue to kill other living beings in all the different plant, animal, bird, and human kingdoms.[171]

There is a rapid increase of interest in psychotropic plants in the modern industrial world. The Indigenous people mostly use psychedelic plants for healing, guidance, and religious ceremonies. These Native cultures treat these entheogenic plants as Sacred Plant Teachers. These plants are not used for fun and recreation. These plants with psychedelic qualities "are the gifts of the gods, if not the gods themselves." It is a new way of looking at these Master Plant Teachers, who are here on the planet to help humanity with mental, emotional, and physical ailments. We are blessed to have them, yet modern humans need to see what a gift they are to us. Ayahuasca has several meanings, and one of them is "vine of the soul," which reveals that this outer reality is just a dream and illusion. The inner reality is more real than the outer. There is a returning back to Source for a deeper understanding of our place in this creation.[172]

Research studies have shown that participants with psychoactive plant teachers had profound changes in their life and that self-love and self-care were prominent. Diet changes, lifestyle upgrades, better choices in friends and past-time activities, improved ability to read people and situations, and the ability to hear the Sacred Plant Teachers were some of the many benefits people from all walks of life shared regarding their entheogen ceremonial mystical experiences.[173]

Entheogen-assisted therapy or psychedelic experiences won't provide the long-term healing effects of the underlying causes while the person is still engaging in alcoholism or drug addiction. They need to be clean and not have any alcohol or drugs, including many prescriptions of psychotropic drugs, in their bloodstream. Their physical bodies need to be pure, and inner work of detox, therapy, and group healing, such as Psychospiritual Integration groups, Alcoholics Anonymous or Narcotics Anonymous, is highly recommended in order for the entheogen to really be able to perform the deep inner healing in the brain, emotional body, and clear trauma stuck in the physical body.[174]

There are many different types of psychedelic research taking place in the United States. Psychedelic research is currently working with people who are smoking and who have anxiety, depression, alcoholism, drug addictions, PTSD, cancer, and end-of-life crisis situations, such as those in hospice care. The entheogenic experience causing a mystical experience for the research participants removes the fear of the unknown after death. Participants have direct first-hand experience with their consciousness and sometimes others on the other side of the veil, which helps them better cope with their life and the stressors of modern life. Once a person has these mystical experiences, the way they look at life is forever changed, and this is proof, due to the way entheogenic participants change their outlook and lifestyle after the experience. It is the participant who decides what to do with these mystical experiences and how meaningful they are to them, and it can take some time to settle in and integrate these new wisdoms.[175]

There are several innovative research projects in many countries that use MDMA (methylenedioxymethamphetamine, street name ecstasy or molly) to treat soldiers with PTSD, since the suicide rates are extremely high. Conventional psychotherapy does not work in treating soldiers suffering with PTSD. "According to official reports, more American soldiers stationed in Iraq and Afghanistan commit suicide because of PTSD than are killed by the enemy." These soldiers return home and try to slide back into our society, yet they are never the same and are expected to forget these memories and just move on. Clinical trials are underway, and as of 2018 in Phase 3, they are having positive results with using MDMA for PTSD treatment.[176] Even the lab-created derivative Ketamine, from the plant Peyote has been shown to cause mystical experiences. While listening to celestial harp music, people had visions of angelic spirits flying in and out of the Earth. As the angelic beings flew in and out of the Earth, they were seen singing, saying over and over how the Earth is deeply loved and they loved the Earth. An impression was left of how the drug has nothing to do with the ability to see the extradimensional reality; it is the plant essence combined with the set and setting (a safe environment with high-vibrational music) that opens up a portal to have mystical experiences. The ordinary reality is just one station listed on Source Frequency Symphony broadcasting station. Infinite Presence within the plant in the right atmosphere allows for the ability to experience another dimensional frequency, causing the travel to other transcendental realities.[177]

Western illnesses are a result of imbalances in the body; another way of putting it is "dis-ease." Our Western medicine sees the physical outcome of illnesses only as a physical breakdown of the human body. Western doctors don't tend to ask the patient about what is going on in their life. Emotional traumas, mental stress, environmental toxins, frustrations, and many others are stored in the body. After so many years, all these restrained and traumatic experiences sit there and fester, energetically poisoning the human body systems. These trapped negatively charged experiences will end up causing mental and physical problems. The energy gets so compacted that it eventually needs to come out and be released from the body. It is believed that the basis of all physical illnesses starts on a mental, emotional, and spiritual level, not on a physical level at all.

Everything is energy, including the physical form, made up of photons, sound, and atomic energy. Entheogens rebalance this energy in the mind and in the body, causing harmony, which brings healing. It seems we are dealing with more psychospiritual causes than just physical factors. Entheogens are psychospiritual medicines that are high-vibrational harmonic sounds that heal the out-of-tune body to the ideal frequencies that the body requires to stay in the level of health energetically. A mystical experience resonates at such a high frequency that it has a transformative effect on all levels: emotionally, mentally, spiritually, and physically. We put a lot of focus on the material reality, whereas we have emotional needs, we need healthy mental environments, positive social interactions that place us in a higher state of well-being. Entheogens help us get back on track, focusing on what we came here to accomplish in this lifetime and rebalancing the energies and flow in the body, which will bring mental and physical health along with spiritual awakening.[178]

What the entheogen or Master Plant Teacher shows the participant during ceremony is their responsibility to integrate into their life. Every participant needs to learn that the entheogen won't do the work for them. The Master Plant Teachers are there to show participants what needs to be looked at or resolved; they show deeper wisdoms and experiences unique and related to each person. The integration process offers the contemplation and action needed by each participant to have a deeper understanding of their identity and a multitude of downloads that will help them while on their physical journey.[179]

All that is within each participant will affect the entheogen journey. A spiritual sage will have a much different entheogen experience and has come to the sacred medicine for spiritual reasons only, as opposed to a participant who has done no inner work, has no spiritual practice, and is only looking to have a good drug trip. The sacred medicine is to be respected, and what lies within each participant will be magnified in order to show them what needs to be shown to them. A person who has a deep, meaningful entheogenic journey can spend a lifetime unpacking all the downloads of information that came to them.[180]

Leaving the physical dimension and traveling to spiritual realms by means of meditation, holotropic breathwork, or entheogenic ceremony will expand one's awareness of what is temporary and what is eternal. The mystical experience transcends the conscious mind, as well as emotional, physical, and social conditioning and other barriers in the physical reality. The spirit realms do not care whether one claims a spiritual belief system or states they have no faith at all; the mystical experience shows that all are Divine Eternal Beings. The mystical experiences provide the opportunity for profound significance and transformation.[181]

There are times when our earthly programming will be exposed and shown to be inaccurate. Entheogens will help the participant to be upgraded in their viewpoints and their unsound beliefs. This opens up grander vistas of the many different forms of expressions seen and unseen that Source will communicate and experience. The entheogens offer a mystical experience from a broader perspective, which can cause a leveling up in the participant's consciousness. There are many manifestations of Source; it is we who place limits on the Infinite Presence. This can quickly cause a transformation of what is really important, and many lifestyle changes and perceptions transpire.[182]

It is easy to judge others for their faults, all the while knowing full well that they also have potential for good deeds. The bad/Darkness makes one appreciate the good/Light. We must walk in Darkness (third-dimensional low reality) for a while in order to really know our true origin is from Source Light Frequency. Many of us have experienced having items stolen from us, and this is a lesson on staying watchful of our personal belongings entrusted to us. In order for anything to manifest in this physical reality, duality must exist; therefore, Light and Darkness are included.[183]

CHAPTER 8

Our Wisdom Is Within

We are taught that all knowledge has to come from outside of ourselves in the outer world. However, our wisdom is within. Yes, we do need to acquire information in the physical world, yet many spiritual truths are hidden in our inner chamber. It may require a spiritual teacher, a guide who has traveled this journey before and can help on this spiritual quest. Be open to spiritual guides as well, such as angelic beings, animal spirits, our spirit guides that walk with us through our human life, ascended spiritual teachers, and even Master Plant Teachers. We assume our only help for guidance is physical people, and yet there is a wide array of beings willing to help us—but we need to ask, for they cannot cross the boundary of our free will. It is our life to live, and we are the artist of our waking dream.

Many times, we forget to ask for help from our spirit guides, angelic beings, nature spirits, and so forth. Let us use our inner guidance system and tap into our inner space. In our busy world we need to set aside time for ourselves to connect with this inner wisdom and hear from our Higher Self. In the beginning it may be hard to hear the Higher Self, with all the distractions, yet with practice it can become second nature. There are different forms of meditation, for instance, a Guided meditation, a Walking mediation where one walks in the forest or park or on a beach, a Riding meditation while riding a bicycle in a peaceful setting or quiet neighborhood, or a Mantra or Singing meditation. Yoga, Chi Gong, and Tai Chi are forms of meditation in movement as well as a Traditional meditation of sitting in a quiet place and spending time going inward. Everyone is unique and will be attracted to different forms of meditation. Meditation brings us inward and connects us with our Divine Essence to feel this union with Source. This connection gives us access to internal wisdom, which guides us daily.[184]

Transpersonal experiences relate to a variety of experiences that a person can have during entheogenic travels. These transpersonal experiences cause a person to go outside of the conscious mind, duality, time and space, the ego, and the personality. These would include stepping beyond "objective reality" and the physical senses. A person during the entheogenic experience comes in contact with loved ones who have crossed over the veil; encounters extradimensional beings; sees events in the future or possible future time lines; meets with different deities, galactic beings, their soul family, past life incarnations, and ancestral lineage; makes a plant and animal consciousness connection; is able to travel to other universes and or galaxies; and experiences Oneness with All, wisdoms from ancient symbols, identification with biology such as atoms, cells, body organs, and so forth.[185]

Dr. Stanislav Grof shares several entheogenic adventures where he felt the experiences were very real and still recalls their vividness to this day. He went to the lowest level to the highest level and shares how he was an atom and then in the center of Source energy. I enjoyed his sharing of another experience where there was a valley and "the river of life flows towards the mouth of God." There was music, and many animals of all kinds, and people who came into this river. How happy, impactful, and deeply inspiring this entheogenic experience was for Dr. Grof. It touched him so deeply, and the impressive experience provided him with experiencing this Oneness with all. One looks at life very differently, and these inspirational entheogenic experiences leave a permanent imprint on one's conscious mind and soul forever. The person had a significant experience, and there is no going back to the way they looked at life before the entheogenic experience.[186]

During a psychedelic experience it was revealed that in one atom, many universes are there that are being experienced and different ways of viewing while in these universes. Each person needs to realize it is important to create an atmosphere that is positive and happy, for this affects the atoms, which are conscious, and will correspond with the same happy or sad outer atmosphere.[187]

Atoms are the energy that all physical objects are made up of and also all nonphysical in energetic form, such as gases, photons, and etheric, which have life and thus Divinity in them. Modern science has stated that life comes from atoms, which make up all visible forms and nonvisible substances to the human eye. The lowest form that consciousness exists in is at the level of each atom. Yes, atoms are sentient beings, and even physicists have come to realize this in experiments, when a person is watching atoms behave in a certain way. The atoms know when another consciousness (the human scientist) is watching them. When cameras are placed in a room to see what happens during an experiment, the atoms act differently. This has been proven over and over to verify this scientific and spiritual truth. To the average person, objects appear to have no life, yet the atoms within that make up any object, whether it is able to move or not, are in constant motion, and since everything is made up of energy/life force, all has the Divine Source Energy within.[188]

Right before the consumption of a sacred Ayahuasca brew, the ego and body are afraid and don't want to let go of control. The Higher Self/Soul is trying to communicate; to bring to the surface; to get the participant's attention of things that need to be cleared out, addressed, or exposed; to identify things that are not for their highest good; to awaken them from the dream; and so forth. If an Ayahuasca participant has done the inner work, then they will be transported to the higher realms for instruction, remembering why they came to earth, providing an overall higher-degree viewpoint, instantly clearing out all the programing, upgrading DNA light codes, checking in with their galactic or celestial light family, clearing ancestral bloodlines of the family tree that they happen to incarnate into from negative energetic karma, and being reminded of their purpose work and for incarnating at this time on earth. These meetings are necessary, and the Higher Self will utilize sacred plant medicines to facilitate these mystical experiences and cause a healing on many levels, answering questions, and bringing an awakening by remembering their true identity of who they were prior to incarnating into physical form. Ayahuasca will not always give you what you want, yet she will give you what you need most.[189]

Our diet, which is called *dieta* in the South American cultures, will play a role in our connection with the entheogenic ingredients. The spirit of the plant will be connecting directly with the soul/spirit of the participant. Once an entheogenic plant is ingested, it stays with them for life and bonds with their DNA. This initiation is an imprint on their Soul and is forever a bond between the Master Plant Teacher and the initiated one. Once this sacred bond has occurred, it is very well known to the initiate. Life is never the same; one has been awakened from their slumber or fully awakened as to a new way of living in this third dimension.[190] DMT (dimethyltryptamine) is common among many plants and is also produced in the brain. DMT is not toxic and not addictive; however, it does provide mystical experiences with the Divine Source that are meaningful and life changing. DMT is a life-altering experience that most participants have stated was very esoteric and changed their worldview.[191]

DMT is at higher levels in the human brain at night while sleeping and is produced by the human body naturally. Why at night? Humans travel to the other side of the veil while sleeping or in the dream state. DMT is considered a very powerful essence because of its ability to open the veil between the different dimensions. DMT is known as the absolute entheogen on this planet.[192] There are several characteristics that are seen in a DMT experience. The participant is beyond the confines or outside of the dimensional time-space continuum; therefore, they are unaware of how long the download of information was received, for it could have been seconds, minutes, and so forth. No time is experienced, and they have a sense that all the information received was a truth that they felt was meant for them. There is a feeling of an indescribable and profound experience. These are characteristics of an entheogenic experience.[193]

There are several people who have contributed to psychedelics research. Bill Richards, a psychologist providing research at Johns Hopkins University, and Roland Griffith, who is a psychedelic pharmacologist researcher also at Johns Hopkins University, currently use psilocybin and LSD in clinical trials on people.[194] A study was done at Johns Hopkins University hospital by Roland Griffiths using psilocybin on cancer patients struggling with depression and anxiety related to end-of-life issues. Psilocybin removed the mental stress of having cancer, and in the clinical trial, in patient questionnaires, patients reported that they had improvement in their overall life outlook. As a result of having the mystical experiences while under the influence of psilocybin/magic mushrooms, their mental health stressors such as a fear of death were removed since they had crossed over the veil and realized there was nothing to fear. These mystical experiences had lasting positive effects.[195]

Our culture has a fear of the unknown of death. A Psychonaut dies to this physical reality each time they go into a psychedelic session and therefore experience a death. If a person were to go into a hypnosis session, most of the time a history of lives lived before this particular life will come up and will be recorded during this hypnotic session to verify that we don't truly die, for death is an illusion. We only die to this physical reality in this recorded historical time period. A participant can learn of these dimensions while in their entheogenic sessions and therefore remember these locations on the other side of the veil after they experience the actual physical death in this reality. Once these other dimensional realities are known, they can go to these spiritual realms after the physical death, for they can remember where they are located and have already experienced being there. Integration is just as important as, if not more important than, the actual psychedelic experience, for it requires dedication to take all the wisdoms gained and apply them directly into one's daily life. Integration is what makes the entheogenic experience lasting, for it changes one's perspective, thoughts, emotions, and actions, which causes the transformational process.[196]

Currently, clinical medical research using psilocybin in end-of-life diagnoses, such as cancer, found in patients having mystical illumination and coming to know of their Divinity that they are eternal life beyond this physical world. There is hope that hospitals and hospices will gain legal approval for end-of-life crisis diagnoses and that entheogens can be provided to help people with a deeper wisdom and comfort of experiencing their inner dimensions. After the mystical experiences, the participants in the psilocybin clinical research described having no more fear of death, and the entheogens provided a gift to enjoy life here more fully while still in this physical reality and the losing of their ego having control over them. Entheogenic participants found that connecting with their Higher Self and Source gave them such comfort and a peace that surpassed all understanding. They came to an esoteric wisdom of there being no before or after birth and death; there is the present moment, and all there is in each moment is Source expressed through them. These entheogenic, ecstatic states of consciousness prove to the individual that their life is eternal and that they live forever. Once awakened, they cannot go back to sleep, and view this temporary life as part of the human journey.[197]

A participant with entheogens under the influence can experience the dying of the ego part of themselves. This is known as having the experience of the "ego death," where an aspect of themselves has died to this physical reality so that they can rise to another level of reality.[198]

When a participant goes through the ego death, they are also experiencing the lower levels of themselves. The participant goes through the ego death first, which is separation from the personality, conscious mind, shadow aspects, and physical form, and then all other deaths in future entheogenic sessions are helping the healing of the collective suffering from many centuries of past tragic history that have taken place against humanity. The Infinite Intelligence knows that this needs to be cleared and will utilize those willing to help with the purging of negative acts and negative energy from this planet, which is a form of healing the collective consciousness.

Discussions have occurred between Psychonaut people who say that they agree that there is a collective clearing and purging they have personally experienced over the many years of entheogenic exploration. These discussions of collective clearing of negative energy resonate with the people who have experienced multiple entheogenic sessions, which is also meant to help in the evolution of humanity on this planet. Participants in psychedelic sessions claim there is this message that is coming through of a transformative nature occurring presently on this planet. There is also an enraptured experience within entheogenic sessions that occurs for the participant, depending upon what is needed for the individual, many times after several sessions of clearing out personal and collective negative energy. This is felt as a deeper connection with the Higher Self. Some participants state that they were able to see their entire life as a Life Review in advance, which suggests that there are experiences in one's life destined as part of their human journey.[199]

To heal the fear allows for the love to come forward and be present in a powerful way that others can see and experience. Many want to deny that Darkness exists within themselves. Not accepting this aspect creates unbalance, for every person has Light and Darkness, higher and lower frequencies, and is experiencing the multiple characteristics of both in their life. There are advantages to going into these darker realms within to gain a better understanding of this observance of ourselves.[200] The journey of healing is not just about having a mystical experience and then everything in one's life is sorted out by itself. We all understand pain and suffering and want to feel whole and happy and integrate the insights into our lives to improve them. Integration is about learning to accept our painful past or current difficulties and move beyond the unhealthy state of being. We can show compassion for others, for we ourselves have experienced pain. Transformation is learning from the Darkness, moving back into the Light by creating opportunities to make a new way of thinking, living, and being.[201]

The ego death is experienced and talked about by people who have entheogenic sessions regardless of what type of entheogen they ingest. There are times when a participant can experience the death of their identity during the entheogenic ceremony, and then the next session, a death experience can happen again. Experiencing the ego death in each session doesn't always occur, for each person is unique. Life and death are big questions and realities for each of us to contemplate.[202] The initiate who has experienced a life-altering change in perception will never be the same.

Humanity is dealing with the absence of sacredness and meaning, and now it has been experienced during the entheogen ceremony. Many initiates during the sacred entheogenic ritual have experienced Source and many other dimensions and are forever changed. Indigenous communities globally have used psychedelics in spiritual ceremony and for healing for thousands of years. It is very normal for the entheogen initiate to have a time of removal of the ego and personality in order for the Higher Self to be able to step forward and provide a higher viewpoint. A remembering is created in this sacred setting where deep insights, vivid visions, and an upgraded view of themselves occur during nonordinary states of consciousness. The shamanic culture views these altered states of consciousness while in ceremony as a healing opportunity to remove the amnesia of people's perception of who they are and their life here. Allowing these nonordinary states of consciousness to be accepted is necessary in the Western culture in order for this process to be a part of the healing and spiritual experience.[203]

We need to die to our belief systems and all that we feel in this material intellectual reality. With each death during a psychedelic session, we are born into a higher reality. At some point, a participant will come to a meeting or a deeper understanding of the Infinite Presence and the overall plan for the galaxies and this local universe. Entheogens don't take us anywhere outside of us but in fact to a deeper level within us and a connection with our inner space.[204]

Jesus and Buddha were human as well and experienced the human journey. We will be evaluated and so must do the best we can do to live our life in the physical form. We tend to put Buddha and Jesus on this high level where we can't attain this level of awareness. There is no need to attend a church to become a highly aware, evolved being. We must follow the footsteps of living a life full of compassion for humanity, as Buddha and Jesus did while they walked this planet.[205]

The Buddha came into Enlightenment and became fully Awake while living in a dense forest for six years. It is possible that Buddha used an entheogenic plant that facilitated a mystical experience causing the Enlightenment. There was no governmental agency saying it was not allowed back while Buddha walked the Earth. Since the beginning of when humans walked this planet, plant intelligence has communicated with Indigenous cultures and was widely acceptable until modern times. Now, entheogens are making their way back to the expansion of acceptance in human consciousness, which will help update the erroneous views of how plants are to be feared. Spiritual teachings are based on love and acceptance of all of life on this planet, and what better way than to feel a deep connection to the fellow human, animal, and plant family? We are all in this together, so we need to value and treasure all living beings that inhabit this planet.

The Buddhistic tradition came from the forest among the plants, which may have talked with Buddha, who was known to have telepathic abilities. Many Buddhists find a bond with Indigenous cultures, for Buddhism respects and honors all life on this planet and believes they are all sentient beings. Then along comes an entheogenic plant and talks with one while in a sacred plant ceremony, and a participant can't forget the messages and all the mystical experiences. Taoism is another spiritual tradition that believes that plants and time in nature should have a reverence for cherishing of these delightful living beings. Spiritual growth is easier to attain in nature than sitting inside a building viewing technology. Yes, technology is needed on this planet, yet spiritual growth is enjoyable with other living beings out in nature. Nature reminds us of life and creates an opportunity for rest, relaxation, and peace.

Mother Ayahuasca is a great teacher and along with other entheogens will cause a transformation of one's consciousness. Ayahuasca is unique in that the purging process releases and heals, energetically and physically, what is needed to be restored in one. Taoism reverence for nature was admired by Chinese Buddhists and later was embraced and assimilated as Zen Buddhism.[206] Gautama Siddhartha, known as Buddha, was living in northern India and came to achieve an awakening, thereby declaring himself as the "awakened one" and coming out of the sleep state or a dreamlike reality. The Sanskrit word for Buddha means "awakened."[207]

There is a strong connection with Buddhism and participants of entheogenic plant ceremonies. Many participants have stated that they experienced the *Bardo*, which is mentioned in the Tibetan Book of the Dead as the lower worlds. The entheogenic participant experiences a separation from the physical body, which allows them to travel to other realms, causing mystical experiences that forever transform their perspective upon returning to the physical world. Having a recognized belief system, such as Buddhism, that talks about these other spiritual realms on the inner confirms what participants state they have personally experienced.

When a participant shares the particular details that match the elements of an insightful and spiritual attainment, the Buddhist tradition has categorized and identified what the entheogenic participant has experienced. For example, the participant will share how they were One and experienced Oneness with all of life, with all the people, plants, elements, deities, stars, planets, and so forth. This is known as Cosmic Consciousness, for the participant has experienced the Divine Connection with everything seen and unseen to the human eye. This mystical experience of Oneness with All will adjust the programming of earthly life to show the true connection and how we are all connected and made of the same spiritual essence, which is Source Itself.[208]

A participant during an entheogenic session needs to be aware that there are realms that they will be visiting and that they may have interaction with beings in that reality. A participant is not allowed to barge right into another realm without respect and protection. These realms have energetic dharmic principles that the participant may not know or understand and therefore may make it difficult to fully engage with this nonordinary reality. These mystical experiences can have the impression of being scary or strange, due to the nature of not being familiar with these dimensions. There are custodians who protect the esoteric wisdoms, and this information is heavily guarded, for only those with a vibration that is high enough will be provided these wisdoms so they will not fall into the wrong hands and be used against humanity or any life on this planet. At any time when a wisdom keeper is opening up these ancient teachings, protection is to be requested before relaying the information; otherwise, it is too risky and can be misused for negative agendas.[209] Ayahuasca was found to intensify and strengthen the Buddhism lifestyle in the Buddhist participants, such as deeper conviction to meditation and staying in the present moment. There is total removal in the connection with death since one travels to the beyond and back through entheogenic mystical experiences.[210]

There are deeper realities, and evolvement never ends. It is a forever journey of self-discovery. The stronger the energy is that a participant comes in contact with, the more they need to ground and integrate, which will allow stabilization. An entheogen participant learns to take this intense "Absolute Light" and live in this new reality.[211] We can go our entire lives, and there is information that won't make it to our conscious level of the mind. Being able to go on an entheogen journey offers an opportunity to reunite with the Higher Self (Soul) to gain deeper wisdoms.[212] At some point in a person's spiritual journey when they move beyond just self-help and are open to self-discovery, the bigger questions will arise. The individual will become interested in realities beyond this dimension, self-realization, incarnation onto this planet, their purpose work, spiritual beings in other dimensions, esoteric teachings from different belief systems, God Realization, and the Divine Plan. Psychology and psychotherapy have their limitations and will refer a person to the religious communities to help in trying to answer these deeper, probing questions. Entheogens answer these deep questions for many participants in the sacred ceremonies.[213]

Many people who have meditated for years without much success have opted to use entheogens by a highly trained facilitator and have gained access to other spiritual realms; hence the ability to have mystical experiences is achieved, which brings more dedication to the spiritual practice of further meditation and spiritual realization. Entheogens enhance spiritual development and spiritual practices. Entheogens cause a new viewpoint while living in the physical world.[214] Mystical experiences are hard to put into a language, and who defines or determines what a mystical experience is? The person will have a deep knowingness, and no one will be able to convince them otherwise. There is a vivid and perfect recall years later of the entire mystical experience, and the sacredness of the events is remembered down to the cellular level.[215]

Entheogens are not drugs. They offer a mystical journey off the physical plane that creates a portal opening into realms to explore, expand consciousness, and realize one's unity with the Divine Essence. Entheogenic plant ceremony initiates from ancient times, including these current times, share "a common Eucharist and theology" of having blessed mystical experiences.[216] A mystic knows there is more than meets the eyes, and this discernment of the physical world is only a small portion of the overall reality.[217] Entheogens were ingested during the Eleusinian religious ceremony by the participants, and what was experienced was more than ecstasy; it was a firsthand revealing of the mystery of one's divine nature and how they are an immortal, eternal, divine being in a physical form.

This would definitely cause a participant to say what happened to them was unspeakable and indescribable.[218] There is a connection between mystical consciousness and entheogenic plants. These plant teachers are so powerful that they have been known to turn an atheist into a person who believes in the Divine and the existence of the Infinite Source.[219]

There are different ways to experience the Divine Presence. Meditation, contemplation, nonordinary states, and so on bring one to these experiences. At some point, a psychedelic participant will experience just being a sphere of light. There is this level of "Diamond Luminosity" of light, and one sees for themselves that this is an aspect of their true identity while in a psychedelic session. Many psychedelic participants meet entities on different levels of reality, yet at some point they will be able to have a direct experience recognizing that they are a Light Being.[220]

There are places that receive sounds not heard by humans that resonate around the planet. When people treat others with love and compassion, it raises the frequency of the person who acted in kindness. Negative actions and thoughts lower the vibrations of the planet, which affects all life on Earth. Currently, the sound frequency is low on Earth. In the beginning, people had telepathic abilities because there was a higher frequency on this planet, and all life would communicate together, work together, live together in harmony. In the very beginning the rocks would talk with humans, the trees would visit with the humans, the animals were playing with the people, and birds would sing and talk with us because humanity was awake, aware, and resonated at a much higher frequency.[221]

While a participant is having an entheogenic experience, there is this feeling that there is a presence with them, guiding them, leading them, showing them information of different kinds. There is also a feeling of familiarity, the importance of this information being relayed to them, the closeness and oneness of everything, the warmth, the feeling of love and other positive attributes known to the participant. There is a sense of expansiveness and yet personal connection of the participant and the spiritual presence and how deeply important it was for them to remember this experience.[222]

When we go deep enough, we reach a paradox. Everything that we see is temporary, and everything that is unseen is eternal. Spiritual instruction has been revealing this spiritual truth for millennia. The Soul puts on the Earth astronaut suit (the human body) and enjoys the journey in a material world on Earth. This hero's journey in the Earth school will provide many experiences while on the human expedition. New Souls are coming to the physical plane daily, and many more have graduated from the Earth school. Classes are taking place at all levels. Some Souls are here at grade levels, and other are completing post doctorate training preparing them for future spiritual assignments in service to the Divine Plan. All Souls are special; some have just been around longer than others, referred to as Old Souls. These mature Souls help the younger Souls by being living examples, by being awake and aware of their spiritual purpose work in this lifetime.[223]

CHAPTER 9

Healing Our Collective Insanity

From a young age Jiddu Krishnamurti was seen as a very evolved Soul. He was born on May 11, 1895, in India and was discovered at a young age by the Theosophical Society founded in the United States. Krishnamurti was seen and educated to be a world leader in the evolution of humankind. Charles Leadbeater was clairvoyant when first seeing Krishnamurti as a young boy on the beach section owned in India by the Theosophical Society; he noticed how pure his aura was and mentioned that it was the brightest he had ever seen. Leadbeater, the leader at that time of the Theosophical Society, decided to educate Krishnamurti to become a spiritual teacher and orator to help advance spirituality on Earth.

Jiddu Krishnamurti gave a speech in 1929 stating that a spiritual path is a pathless approach and religions should not force people on a particular path. A person should only follow Truth, not another person, and a teacher should only be focused on setting people free from beliefs, mental cages, fear, and mental programming. Krishnamurti broke away from the Theosophists on the day he gave his speech on August 3, 1929. He did not want to be a religious or philosophy leader, as he was focused on setting people free and denounced all organized belief.

Shamans free people from the confines of their beliefs and through mystical experiences show the experiencer what lies within, which is our Divinity. When one awakens to this Truth, they become their own shaman, spiritual mastership has arrived, and there is no one to give their devotion to, causing them to give their power away. A spiritual master will step away from organized belief systems and will step out into the landscape of their life with the freedom to be the artist of their life's canvas. The mastership lies within each of us, and it is up to each individual to recognize this and then move in this direction. The path is within, not outside of one, and the steps to mastership are also within. A spiritual teacher just points the way, is a guide, yet each Soul needs to take the journey inward to discover this Divinity for themselves and can have a direct experience.[224]

During a hypnosis session she was conducting, Delores Cannon, a hypnotherapist, had received this answer from the Higher Self of the client. It is revealed that the more awake and aware a person is, the more they are evolved and come to know their true "God identity," which causes more evolution.[225] Entheogens are teaching the participants that all have the Divine Essence Within and can remove the boundaries between cultures and people. It has been mentioned that the entheogens can heal the brokenness of humanity, fear-based thinking, and destructive behaviors of greed, power, and gain over all living beings on this planet. Entheogens facilitate authentic mystical Oneness with the Divine.[226]

Entheogens need to be respected, and participants need to not take too much at one time. Peyote, like many other entheogens, will remind the participant of their Divinity by having a mystical experience with the Divine Essence. This mystical experience will cause an awakening to a higher reality. Integration is very important, for sometimes the participant can get despondent when coming back to living in a denser materialistic level and the emptiness of a world consumed with capitalism. The visionary plants awaken one from a dream life of feeling they are just on a treadmill with no meaning. When a participant visits the realm of the Supreme Creator, beholds their Divinity, and learns of their purpose work or why they came into physical form, it can be very overwhelming.

The entheogens will lead a participant back Home. One knows they have experienced Source Frequency. The celestial bliss is forever held in one's being. A person can no longer be misled into believing this physical reality as real; they instead see the physical world as only one of many dimensions. When a person has a direct mystical illumination, they are no longer deceived by the perceptions of the material world and have become enlightened to a mystical consciousness. The entheogens have introduced them to their Higher Self, the Source within, and their Divinity has been revealed. The participant comes back to the material world and no longer feels they are a mere mortal. When one has seen their Divinity inside their inner planes, they walk among the masses and on the Earth differently.[227]

Our modern culture is unaware of what the wisdom keepers called shamans are seeing, what is happening right under our noses, and us modern folks are too mesmerized to be watchful of what we assume is for our best interest. Multinational corporations view natural resources and human resources as tools to control the level of consciousness of the population into believing they need all these materialistic goods, which end up in wasteland dumps piled so high that there are huge mounds of them covered with grass and pipes sticking out to allow for the toxic gases to escape. Our societies around this precious planet are hypnotized into this perpetual enslavement of capitalism. We believe our savior is consumerism, transhumanism, and all the institutions that have been put in place only to suppress our freedom of exploration into the inner planes, which distracts us from what is lasting, eternal, and beneficial for all. This is the call for those willing to hear of how our global economics have created a vacuum inside people who are desperate to fill this void with the latest amusements of all kinds. The Gnostic Christians of the first centuries AD talked of Archons, who are spiritual entities that have negative influence over our physical third-dimensional world and the human minds. We are seeing the effects of runaway capitalism on all the living beings on this planet. Deeper wisdoms need to come forward and be introduced into all the collective society systems. Global destructive empires are the result of spiritual emptiness, isolation, lack of community, corporate corruption, and greed, all as a result of demonian-type, callous ways of thinking and living. We cannot continue this way, as if all will work itself out, all on its own accord. Shamans and the plants have the power to remove this insanity from our minds and provide the necessary healing to humanity and the planet, causing a beneficial vision for our future. By healing our collective insanity first, new updated systems can then be put in place that are not corruptible. We cannot rely on someone else to save us; we need to step up and transform our view by recognizing our own Divinity and godly power, for this is the dimension we have been placed in to transform and to take personal responsibility. As Eternal Divine Beings, we have the power to wake up, break free from the collective mind control of feeling we have no power, expose the deceptions, and remove ourselves from this sleep state of being. Could it be that the plants are trying to awaken us? To show us through mystical experiences a higher, more peaceful existence with all of life on this planet? The plant kingdom is working on our behalf, and the animal kingdom is waiting for humanity to realize all are sentient beings and for us to live as Divine Beings.[228]

The icaros is a song each vegetalista shaman sings out loud when healing, creating entheogenic mystic brews, and in ceremony. Icaro is the sound of creation placed into words and with a musical tone sung by the vegetalista shaman. This creative sound comes from the cosmos, and everything is manifested by this primordial sound. We come from the stars, yet we are connected to Gaia, our nurturing mother, since our physical bodies are made from her earth substance. We are one with all life, and being physical helps us realize we are a part of the cosmos, planets, and all living beings in the universe. Source is all and we are an aspect of Source learning all these great wisdoms while in physical form.[229]

Love and Hate are the duality we all face within ourselves. There is an "awakening process" where one comes to know that love is the truest expression of Source and fear is an expression that is just further away. Love provides the happiness to be conveyed outward to all, and this helps heal the fear in the collective.[230]

Entheogens and psychedelics "reliably produce spiritual or mystical experiences." Research questionnaires from participants and general conversations with participants of entheogenic substances confirm on a consistent basis the mystical experiences that cause life transformations. Whether inside or outside research environments, all one has to do is just go onto the internet and look up entheogens or psychedelics testimonials to see the transformative power of this psychospiritual medicine. When a participant has crossed the veil and been to the other side of life, the individual is never the same. There are certain characteristics such as feeling the connectedness to everything in the universe, no fear of death, Divine Union, and a sense of a greater purpose of a magnificent system.

In the entheogenic community, it is believed that the mystical experience itself is what causes the metamorphosis and healing. Humanity has a right to have mystical experiences in a safe and sacred setting so they can access their remembering of their true, divine identity, which will be the catalyst for the continued existence of human beings and all other life on this planet. Ongoing psilocybin research at Johns Hopkins Hospital has proven that the research participants have mystical experiences, and according to data, the descriptions of images and experiences were the same as documented ancient mystics' experiences. It was also reported that health improved in both the modern and ancient entheogenic participants.

Humanity not knowing their true identity as a Divine Being, and thus feeling separate from all the seen and unseen, is on a path leading toward a great reduction of the human species due to war, hatred, corruption, and so forth. We have different forms of life who have already experienced complete extinction on this planet. It is believed that entheogens and psychedelics can place humanity back onto a better path because of the fact that participants become ecologically conscious of this divine connection with everything. Sacred plant ceremony participants are especially more involved in environmental concerns and actively engage in ecology projects to reverse the damage to this large biodiversity of life on this precious, beautiful planet.[231]

In medical entheogenic clinical research projects that are taking place, the participants are asked to share their experiences with the entheogen, on a questionnaire. Mystical experiences most often occur, which are the cause of profound lifestyle changes and perspectives. A description of an entheogen on a medical research questionnaire by a participant revealed her magnificent mystical experience of Oneness with Source. This entheogen research participant also was shown Source's impression of humanity. She shared of seeing so much destruction by humanity to all of life on this planet. Liken this to a parent watching a hurt child act out their anger, standing there ready to provide compassion, yet knowing the child will one day evolve emotionally and spiritually. During her entheogenic mystical experience, this participant shared Source's panoramic observation: "Utmost love and pity and compassion for all those suffering souls unable to see beyond their own senses, their feelings, their lusts and desires, their machines of destruction, their wars, hates and jealousies, their bodies, their five little senses. Profound love." The entheogen research participant reconnected to the Oneness with the Infinite Presence in order to observe humanity from an off-planet viewpoint.[232]

At some point in the human evolution, we will be able to remember our true identity and keep the connection to the Infinite Presence on this side of the veil. Once humanity has upgraded our collective consciousness to a higher level, we will be able to sustain the "coherence" necessary to stay in union with Source.[233] Belief systems that are open for self-exploration create an opportunity for self-expansion, to be able to use spiritual practices along with entheogens to enhance connection with the Divine and remember one's internal connection with Source. Much can be learned in the darkness on the far side, out of view, to have a deeper understanding that we chose to come into a dark world and shine our light. One can't appreciate the Light unless they have experienced Darkness. Not knowing brings one in search for what is wanting to be known hidden deep on the inner planes of one's own being.[234]

The holy sacrament given to Eleusis Mysteries initiates was a psychoactive visionary elixir. Wanting converts, the early Christian Church included an entheogen in both the bread and the wine and called it their communion with God, deemed the sacramental Holy Eucharist. The evidence between the two is striking, for psychedelic plants were known in these cultures, so in the Last Supper Eucharistic ceremony Jesus was sharing the psychedelic bread and wine, which was also used in the Eleusis Mysteries in Greece. Grinding entheogenic plants into powders and placing them as an ingredient into a drink or food is a practice that had been done for centuries in many cultures around the world. Jesus was sharing this Eleusis Mystery with his 12 apostles at their Last Supper together. Sharing this secret with the apostles or another spiritual ceremony either way would ensure new converts a new way of living and a new path.

As the Christian Church grew over time, in later years it would deny its entheogenic Eucharistic sacred roots. If Christians today could have an entheogenic Eucharist communion ceremony and thus have a life-altering mystical experience of other dimensions and see their own Divinity, outside the confines of Christianity, then they would bypass the intermediator of church organizations. People would be able to have the mysteries of life solved, Divine Union, and not just hear about spiritual topics but have direct personal experience. Humanity is now looking for more than just words; they want the mystical experience, which explains why entheogens are resurfacing in the modern cultures.[235]

The Eleusis ceremony was a once-in-a-lifetime event to experience. All Eleusis participants would have mystical experiences that were ineffable. A person had to experience it, and only then would they understand the significance of a sacred plant ceremony, which would bring deep insights and a higher knowingness of their true identity of union with Source. How could one speak of such mystical wisdoms? It has been revealed that hallucinogens were used in the

Eleusis religious ceremonies.[236] An entheogen mystical experience will many times have a unity consciousness encounter, causing an illuminated state of understanding that is interconnected with everything. There is also union with the Infinite Presence and a realization of one's True Identity of being Divine and being a god, for the Soul is made up of 100 percent Source. Self-Realization and God Realization have occurred during an entheogen mystical experience by participants, causing a transcendental awakening of their true identity that forever changes them and how they live their life. This is why addictions fall away, fear of death is removed, and a new way of viewing and living is created in this physical world.[237]

Entheogens reveal our Divinity and Oneness with Source. It's criminal to take away people's liberties for self-exploration with the use of sacred entheogens, for this keeps them away from this remembering of their Divine Essence. There is a transformation that takes place with an entheogenic ceremony that causes a mystical experience that changes their vision for life here and on their inner planes. This is a mystical state of being.[238] Psychospiritual medicine deepens one's connection with the Divine Essence by showing them their connection with the entire universe. How can one go back to a view that all there is to life is just physical? Many participants who have taken plant medicines report how they have an expanded view as a result of being exposed to different spiritual realms. They now see the Divinity in both the visible and invisible worlds.[239]

Many people are raised in households where they were not loved and felt unloved as children. Now these children are adults and still feeling unloved. Over and over during integration circles where participants share their entheogen experiences in order to help in the process of applying the wisdoms into their daily life, the overpowering feeling of being completely loved comes up. This experience of feeling completely and deeply loved is a state of bliss. Union with the Divine, these Sacred Plant Teachers facilitate between a Soul and the Infinite Presence being expressed as being divinely enraptured by love. So many Souls go through life feeling unloved, and then a wise entheogenic plant comes into a person's life and shows them how special and loved they are, how divine they are, and how they are one with Source for they are an aspect of Source. This is the power of these Master Plant Teachers. They have the power to show us who we are as divine beings having a human journey.[240]

Earth is a school, and one of the many lessons for Souls is "to teach us to know good from bad." In a duality-based third-dimensional plane, there has to be Light and Darkness. A Soul is easily tempted to go toward Darkness as opposed to the Light. Before they incarnate Souls will say they will work for the Divine Plan and for the Light, yet all are tested in the Earth School, and because they are asleep and not awake, they fail many exams. These students don't want to hear spiritual truths because they would rather drown themselves in the circus of the world.

Our voice has power; it can bless or curse others by our spoken words, starting as a conscious thought. Unawake people are unaware of their negative thought forms and negative words toward others. The deception is prominent among the population, for they are no longer able to tell the difference between truths and fallacy. The world is on a path of destruction if nothing changes. Everyone feels deep down that what we are doing to the planet and to all living beings on it is not sustainable. What good is all this wealth if it's not shared with others? All the resources on this planet are for everyone equally, not a select few to hold on to and only use for themselves.

Violence is at an all-time high, and people have become desensitized to the feelings of others. We live in such a lonely society, yet no one has time to talk at length with each other. Humanity is at a pivotal point on this planet. If things continue as they are, we will see the collapse of all these corrupt systems in order for new balanced systems that are in harmony with natural law and spiritual law. We know things have to change by upgrading and raising the vibrational level on this planet. Many people are working toward this goal, yet there are more asleep at the wheel than there are others who are awake and driving responsibly with their eyes wide open. Handing the keys to expensive cars to children does not teach the characteristics of kindheartedness, sensitivity, empathy, benevolence, service to others, humility, philanthropy, generosity, and so many more that would benefit all living beings on this planet.

The mass corruption and cruelty toward others can't continue, for we all will perish on this planet. The plants are saying to the vegetalista shamans that the hearts of humanity need to move toward love of all life living here. Many say the plants are "the voice of God" trying to get our attention and wake us up. "We are gods, too, but we do not know how to take our proper place as gods." It all comes back to plants. We cannot live without them, for they feed us and provide the vital gift of oxygen for all living beings. The Divine Essence lives within all the vegetation on this planet and was here first, long before humans and animals were placed here. Where there are no plants, there is no life.[241]

Master Plant Teachers will sometimes show a hard love in order to teach the entheogen participant difficult truths to swallow, causing a leveling up and acceptance of their spiritual royalty position. Once a person comes to the realization of their Divine level, this awakening causes a stepping into their Higher Self and the beginning of living the best expression of Source. A person will feel the power of being an embodiment of Source in physical form, which then causes a sense of commitment to serve the Divine Plan. There comes a higher awareness of why they incarnated on Earth. We are all a piece of Source Essence and therefore all one in the same as magnificent eternal Souls.

The physical body is only a temporary vessel housing the Soul, yet the glorious Soul expands beyond the cosmos. All there is that exists is Source, so Soul being an aspect of the Infinite Presence surpasses all time, space, and physical realms. The notion of separation is illusion, for we as Souls are made 100 percent of Source and are only limited while in physical form. Thereupon, the suffering comes as a result of incorrect perception, and only in the physical reality does it appear that we are separate beings in order to experience what separation is like and individuality.

It does not mean that we lose our uniqueness when we cross over the veil; after leaving this physical life, it means we had an opportunity to express our uniqueness separate from all other energetic forms. This is why it is called the veil of forgetfulness, for we forget that we are all one when we incarnate into form and yet energy all comes from Source. The Divine Source separates Itself into different pieces without diminishing Itself to experience life on many different dimensions. That is how spectacular each Soul is to Source, for it is Source Itself. When we come to the place where this is realized, we are restored, remembering our true heritage, and we are fully awake. There is no you; there is only Source. This is your true identity and creates true healing from the egoic world of the physical plane.[242]

In 1 Corinthians, it states how the human body is the temple that houses the Divine Source. There is a wonderment when a person travels inward to find this Infinite Presence and to see their own Divinity. "Do you not know that you are God's temple and that God's Spirit dwells in you?"[243] We are Divine royalty, 100 percent filled with Source Magnificent Light Frequency. Entheogenic mystical experiences reveal our true identity as godlike beings. We incarnated to experience form and the human journey filled with many physical experiences.[244] Source shows Itself in so many varieties of ways. All one has to do is step out into nature. This is Divinity on display. When one realizes that they are one with source, then they are one with nature.

All are One and One are All. Only the mind sees separation, and this is why the material world is an illusion. All that you see is the conscious mind in what is called the Waking Dream. Source is the Eternal Dreamer, and all is Source experiencing this adventure we call life. It may seem like a paradox, yet in duality (the dual worlds) in the mental planes, where the physical plane resides in the mental dimensions, one is seeing the universal mind power in action. A person is also seeing Source, for all including the Mind (conscious, subconscious, and higher mind) has been created by Source as well.[245]

CHAPTER 10

The Wake-Up Call to a Higher Reality

The Soul in the human form has a longing for knowledge (gnosis) of its true identity as union with Source. There is a veil between what humanity perceives in the physical world and Divine Source, which reveals the mystical unity. The Soul of the human knows there is a mystery to be solved and begins the spiritual quest. The Soul on this journey comes to realize this Infinite Presence is within all that is seen and unseen. A veil is between what humanity perceives in the physical world and the Divine Source, which reveals the mystical union. All of Source will help the Soul solve this mystery and will use the unseen aspects of Itself, such as Creator Intelligence in the plants, to create the understanding of Soul's Divinity through mystical experiences. Gnostic and Hermetic writings share of these "mystic enlightenment and spiritual rebirth" teachings discussing the power of this celestial Divine Essence and Soul's discovery of its spiritual royalty. An awakening takes place, also referring to a rebirth or enlightenment as to one's true identity; the Soul now has solved the mystery and accepts its majesty with Source, for it is formed from Source Itself.[246]

Source is within each of us, wearing a disguise as a human form. It is the ego, the personality, the shadow, and the physical form—all aspects of the mind. We are in the reality of the mind in the physical plane. This is the reality of emotions, thoughts, physical senses, psychic abilities, memories, the recognition of form and colors, the intellect for learning information, and the sense of separation from other forms. A spiritual master will be able to see beyond the outer covers of the mind that cover the Soul/Source within each person, no matter what their outer personality and behavior show in the outside world. We have mental diseases that cause suffering to others, such as greed, apathy, narcissism, lust, prejudice, judgment, self-absorption, attachment, and vanity, to name a few. These are diseases, or, as the Yogis of the East would say, the passions of the conscious mind. The spiritual master will see these outer reflections as the mind and not the Soul/Source.

The mind is needed in the lower dimensions, such as the third dimension of physical reality. It is the mind that has to drive the car to the supermarket, pick out the food, complete the financial checkout process, drive back home, and handle all aspects of physical, emotional, and mental life for the individual. The problem is we believe we are all these coverings and forget the true identity as the luminous eternal Soul that powers all the aspects of the conscious mind. The unawake person will see these mental diseases/passions of the conscious mind as darkness, wrong, sin, corruption, wickedness, deviltry, and decay of a person's mental state of being to cause suffering to others. We begin to see that the other person has been made ill and controlled by negative aspects of their conscious mind. We have been fed negative news, violent movies, argumentative television, and suffering in unsympathetic media and societal systems that regulate the population.

The conscious mind can become unhappy, depressed, and angry at all the situations caused by this lower-vibrational third dimension. The conscious mind is a separate conscious aspect, and because a person is not their mind, for they are a Soul, this is why the ancient Hindu teachers would say befriend the mind. Be aware of this aspect of you. Yes, the conscious mind is here to help, yet it can be your friend or foe, for it is dual in nature. The conscious mind is a good servant yet a terrible master.[247]

Harmonic sound frequencies from Source Frequency are Soul/ Higher Self, and only an aspect of this is in human form. We can travel into a glorious realm to familiarize ourselves with our true essence. Our consciousness affects us and affects the outer world in this collective, for we are knitted together. It is our personal lower worlds from where we have come to view the overall state of affairs, experience physical form, provide an assessment, accomplish our preset goals, and remember our Divinity, a true state of beingness. Entheogens wake us up to a higher reality and an out-of-the-ordinary reality for a quick emergence out of the sea in order to view the sky and sun. We spend so much time under the water that it's like a fish that flies out of the water to take a look at the reality above only to then splash back underneath, yet it remembers seeing all that was viewed above.[248]

Since the Divinity is within each of us, we can start to have interactions that promote this ability to recognize each other on a Soul-to-Soul basis and way of living. There are friendly reminders each day to help cultivate a lifestyle of remembering there is a Soul within each person we meet. Even difficult interactions can be viewed as just the person's conscious mind acting out in a negative way, and we don't have to take it personally. We are also not a doormat and need to set healthy boundaries. There is no place that Source is not. It is the conscious mind that is covering Divinity. A smile is a good way to start every interaction. I will give you an example of the power of giving a smile to someone.

One day, I went to an outlet shopping center in the Orlando, Florida, area. I lived at the time 1.5 hours away from this outlet center and decided to make a day of it. After I had purchased some items, I went to lunch. The restaurant greeter at the front door saw me come in, and in my usual style, I smiled at her and said hello. I thanked her for seating me and wished her well. I enjoyed my meal, and on the way out, I acknowledged the greeter again with a smile and wished her a lovely day. I did not think anything further as I drove back home. Two months later I realized there were another few items I needed that could be purchased at this outlet shopping center in the Orlando area. Once again, I drove to Orlando, went to the outlet, and then went to the same restaurant, for they had a menu of meals with fresh vegetables.

As soon as I walked in the door, the same greeter was at the front entrance greeter station. The first thing that came out of her mouth was "You are back!" I was taken by surprise, for I was amazed that after two months she remembered me, especially after she must have seen large amounts of people vacationing in the Orlando area, for this restaurant was near all the Orlando attractions and amusement parks. I quickly responded, "How did you remember me? For there are so many people who must have come in here since I was here." She said, "Because you smiled." I was shocked! I responded, "People are on vacation in this area of Orlando, and surely they are happy and would be smiling." The greeter shared, "They never smile at me. I am just the person who seats them at their table. People are not happy, even on vacation." She remembered me because of my smile coming into the restaurant and the fact that I acknowledged her on my way out as I was passing her greeter station area. She was so happy to see me again and experience the warmth of a smile.

Never underestimate the power of a friendly smile. When I go to the grocery store or any store, I like to say hello and smile at each staff person working who is putting out items. Many times, I will come into conversation and try to remember their name. It's a habit of mine, and the staff then starts coming over to say hello to me when they see me come into their section of the store. I visit the same stores, so I get to know all the staff, and, in some cases, I get hugs. I talk about what is new with them and take an interest in how they are doing. If I am out at a restaurant, a person who works at a store I visit to purchase items will remember me and stop by my table to say hello, even after they don't work at that store anymore.

There are so many people who work at stores where I shop, and I don't remember everyone, yet they remember me for how I would interact with them and the other staff members. There is an expression that goes, "Are people happy when you enter the room? Or are they happy when you leave the room?" Think about that. People observe more than you realize. Each living being, whether human, animal, plant, or rock, is Source just vibrating at a different frequency and showing up in a different form. Be creative and practice remembering that all is Source.[249]

At some point in the entheogenic experiences, a participant comes to realize there is no other than themselves, which is the Higher Self within these sessions. Once a participant goes to the nondual reality level, it is perceived that there is no outside. When a person is in duality, there is them and there are others, a separateness between themselves and everything else. Now, when a participant moves into expansive inner space within themselves, they can come in contact with other entities, and a larger picture or history is explained to them. We are the microcosmos of the macrocosms.

Entheogenic sessions are a journey into one's inner being. Thousands of years and the overall story of humanity can be shown or downloaded to the participant while in ceremony. There are entities that are so massive that they are the size of galaxies. "Millions-of-light-years-across beings, and these were the beings that were responsible for generating time and space itself and the formative conditions within time and space." These beings can reach out to connect with participants to teach, explain, initiate, and encourage them while they are on their current mission on earth in their physical human form to help humanity during this transformative time.[250]

In the *Republic* by Plato, there is a parable of the cave where prisoners are required to stay by chains together. They have nothing to do but watch the movement of half-light shadowed projections of forms on the high cave wall. The prisoners perceive this to be the only reality, their "real world." These projections are created by people using puppets behind a screen with a fire as the light providing the ability to cause the perception of a true and only reality to the prisoners. The puppeteers are the architects of the prisoners' complete reality. The prisoners know nothing of the reality outside the cave.

One day a prisoner was able to escape from the chains and left the cave, only to find a beautiful reality of natural landscapes, rivers, abundance of colors, flowers, the magnificent sun, stars, other beings, and a completely different reality. The freed prisoner comes to discover the puppeteers, the fire, and the veil that covers and hides the true reality from the chained prisoners in the cave. Now that the freed prisoner has seen a grand reality outside of the cave, he transforms into a "philosopher king" and decides to return to the cave and deliver the wisdoms of this exquisite luminescent, bright, and vast reality.

The Awakened prisoner comes back to the dark cave and offers to free the chained prisoners so they can experience this reality gloriously filled with light. The prisoners who have lived their whole lives in the dark cave think the freed Awakened One is crazy with bizarre ideas and can't fathom a reality outside of the cave. They feel safe and content in the darkness of the cave. The prisoners believed the Awakened One was blinded by the light, causing him confusion in discerning which reality was real. The Awakened One was convinced that the true reality was indeed outside of the darkened cave. Therefore, all the prisoners declared it was illegal and banned anyone from being able to leave the cave, for it causes this confusion over which reality is the real one.

The prisoners didn't believe the Awakened One and instead self-policed in the cave so no one could leave and get confused. The Awakened One is destined to live amid the unawake and spend the rest of life progressively teaching and providing an opportunity to the prisoners to receive enlightenment to an eternal reality. This allegory that was written by Plato, who died around 348 BC, still causes an awareness today for those who have left the cave, expanded their consciousness, and experienced enlightenment through a mystical experience. Anyone who has ingested entheogens, or had a deep mystical experience, can relate to Plato's parable about the cave. It was very well known that Plato was an initiate of the Eleusis Mysteries in Greece, where the psychedelic *kykeon* was served to the participants during the sacred initiation. The awakening takes place of other realities and a different perspective of their physical reality once the participant arrives back after the completion of the entheogenic ceremony.[251]

Those who have experienced extradimensional realities not only have an awakening but also are seen as in an alternate reality or seen beyond the veils that the human culture has overlaid upon us. Entheogens have this power to offer mystical experiences, expand consciousness, and travel to strange realities filled with other beings inhabiting all these realms. Our modern society does not appreciate or fully understand these Master Plant Teachers, this plant intelligence that has been on this planet long before humans walked the Earth. Those Souls who have experienced these nonphysical dimensions are considered odd, out there, foolish, and strange, for the current society does not know how to relate to these aware individuals of these other realities.

These people feel the modern culture has set them aside, has ridiculed them, and may even distain or have aversion to them. Mystical experiences are unique, and not all are positive, and not all are negative either, yet when a person has experienced extradimensional realities, it is not forgotten and no one can convince them these were not real. These Souls that have traveled beyond the veil of forgetfulness are forever transformed, and many state that the mystical experience was one of the most impactful experiences in their life.

The Souls that have been awakened by experiencing these other dimensions walk among the general population, yet they are more aware of the inner workings of nonmaterial realms. We have always had individuals walking the Earth, awaken, aware, and who have interacted with these ethereal dimensions. The time has come to welcome these personal tales of explorations in these unworldly vistas and garner what they have learned and experienced directly.[252] A profound wisdom is shared during deep mystical entheogenic experiences. We can call and reference this Divine Intelligence, yet it can be called by many names; however, Source is experiencing itself. Once union with the Divine has been experienced, a person goes into a state of longing; it is so painful and at times excruciatingly as a state of agony.[253]

After sacred entheogenic experiences, a participant is in between two worlds. They step away with these incredible and many times profound wisdoms received; they also have been in other dimensions, and now that their feet are back on the earth, they are wondering how they are going to integrate all this into their life. Now that the mystical experiences have occurred, the participant is never the same and can never see life the same, which causes deep, meaningful insights and therefore deep changes internally and externally. Love is the true reality, and anything outside of this is an apparent perspective reality, a particular viewpoint. Love is the foundational power that drives all realities. There is just an overlay on top of this Primordial Love Frequency reality that is seen as a matrix, and then the participant discovers and experiences the true reality in a sacred entheogenic session.

Having direct experience with this Infinite Loving Presence is life changing, and there is no going back to the old way of existing in this life. Now, what does one do with all this after the mystical experience? Psychedelics are here to help us as a sacred medicine and as an important part of healing humanity—the birthing of a new humanity, coming out of the darkness and living in the light. The entheogenic experience is a returning to a mystical state and a remembering of our Oneness, which is each other. The participant is given wisdoms of why they came here and are to be of service to humanity.

We are at a turning point on this planet. Will humanity work together, or will humanity have to destroy more to see that cooperation is the way where everyone benefits in healing the planet and each other? The hope is that humanity won't turn away from what is hurting this planet and everything that lives here. Humanity can turn toward the light or can be the generation that ends much of life on this planet, due to the law of free will that is allowed on Earth. Many scholars, researchers, scientists, mystics, Psychonauts, and so forth are wanting to see entheogens removed from the restricted Schedule 1 classification to offer the public access to these for hospice care, including cancer patients and medically safe retreat centers for exploring consciousness. It will allow more open research projects to further learn of all the potential healing treatments emotionally, mentally, and physically for humanity.[254]

Entheogens boost the neurotransmitters and receptors in the brain while reducing the traumatic remembrances and the Default Mode Network in the cerebrum. Psychotropic plants improve communication throughout the brain and provide higher levels of the more than 40 neurotransmitters in the brain; a few that do the majority of the work are serotonin, gamma-aminobutyric acid (GABA), dopamine, glutamate, norepinephrine, acetylcholine, and histamine. The Default Mode Network within the brain is believed where someone feels they are a separate person, which can cause a sense of separation, loneliness, depression, and negative thought patterns replaying. Psychoactive plant medicines lower the operation of the Default Mode Network, which brings in this feeling of Oneness with everything and, for many, Oneness with their Sacred Essence.

Mystical illuminations, such as their Infinite Soul, are fully aware of the higher realms, and their circumstances are temporary, yet they are Eternal, a remembrance of their Divinity and that they are an embodiment of the Source Power, and many other realizations. When a person has a deep mystical experience, the mundane life or physical memories are viewed more from a higher perspective, as if attending the Earth school lessons. Entheogenic participants have shared how all the cultural programming was exposed and they felt free from all the confines of modern social messages, living their life with a viewpoint of how their human incarnation benefits them on the Soul's journey and recognizing the difference between this conscious life and the transcendental realms within them, experiencing an initiation into the deeper levels of one's consciousness. Crossing the veil into these non-physical dimensions, connecting with Source, remembering of their Divinity and Oneness with this Infinite Presence allow for healing to occur on all levels, and their life purpose in this life is revealed. Once Self-Realization and God Realization have been reached, they will always remember their true identity as an embodiment of Source.[255]

A Soul needs intimacy with the Infinite Presence as an actual experience. The conscious mind can only take one so far, and then a mystical experience will provide the wisdoms from the sacred encounter. This is not an objective outer reality; it is subjective experiential inner reality mystical experience.[256] The mystery schools of the ancient past are gone, yet not the sacred knowledge that was hidden, for only those initiates who could understand would later become teachers and pass the information down to a select few of their students.

The time has come for this sacred knowledge to be accessible for all people who are interested and want to learn these ancient teachings. We have moved into a new era, which is raising the energy of the planet, which also affects humanity living on Earth. The raising of the energetic harmonic frequencies in humans' bodies causes humanity to be more aware and awake and to understand these ancient teachings. These sacred teachings are now accessible to the masses, and humanity is waking up to a level to be able to appreciate and garner these once esoteric hidden wisdoms.[257]

Many Souls have incarnated to the Earth at this time to help with the raising of the consciousness on this planet. These are awakened Souls, or Souls becoming awakened, that came here to help in this energetic transition on Earth. The harshness on this low and very dense vibrational planet is very hard on these evolved Souls that came to help humanity. These "Star Children" feel this planet is a strange world where humanity is irascible, illogical, and unpredictable, for they are mostly ruled by their emotions, which can shift at any moment. The cruelty to others is so painful for these evolved Souls that came to help during this shift in consciousness. Most of the evolved Souls don't want to be here and will say how this life on Earth is much harder than expected.[258]

Many of the evolved Souls that came to Earth during this transition where humanity's consciousness will be elevated are here for this mission. The evolved Souls are here to do energetic work similar to a human transformer, where the energy comes in very high and they step down the energy in order for humanity to be able to receive it. This allows for the ability to continually raise the frequency on the planet and set this higher vibration on Earth. These evolved Souls are sent by Source to Earth to serve the Divine Plan.[259]

Many signed up for this assignment on Earth to help humanity during this transitional time of the current collective to a higher positive energetic level of humanity. For the sacrifice that we give during our assignments down here on Earth, we will find that it was all worth what we went through during our lifetime. Once the shift in human consciousness finally changes to a higher vibrational frequency, the humans that are birthed on planet Earth will be a new type of human. Our sacrifice will come with blood, sweat, and tears, yet the future upgraded human will be a majestic being.

There is a removal of a "sense of privacy" where a person can be deceptive and take from others when in fact there is no separation. Humans will come to learn that when there are humans starving, then it affects all of humanity, for the human collective will be cohesive and will feel the pain of others starving. This will be so painful that it will stop occurring where some humans can take from others and not be able to hide behind the veil of secrecy and privacy. Full transparency and heart-filled consciousness will be the new collective humanity, and this will change the lives of all who live on this planet.

A "Diamond Light" and a "Diamond Soul" will be the new upgraded humanity characteristics. This new upgraded humanity will remember their true identity as an aspect of Source and utilize this new intelligence to fix the problems on this planet. This Diamond Soul will retain its full identity as Source in physical form and will keep this connection with Source while in this physical form living on this planet. As long as humanity feels we are separate from each other and what we do to each other does not matter, we will continue to see the collective suffer from this low-vibrational mentality. When humanity starts to work in unity and with cooperation, then there will be a birth of a new magnificent humanity.[260]

CHAPTER 11

Empathogens Generate Connectedness and Transformational Processes

Humanity is now starting to wake up to remember who they are, that planet Earth is just a temporary visit to a school, and they are Divine Beings. These Master Plant Teachers (Plant Medicines) help remove the veil of forgetfulness, and the mystical experiences are more real than this lower third-dimensional reality. Third density is dream-like compared to the experiences on the other side of the veil. These entheogens are Healers, and a Psyche Surgery takes place where the veil is lifted and much is revealed. The revelations occur during the ceremonies. The healing occurs afterward in the Integration process.

Hallucinogens offer changes in consciousness during the experience that show visions, images, and sensations. Cannabis/cannabinoids, known as marijuana, that contain the psychoactive agent THC offer neurological, physical, and psychological benefits and provide a feeling of being high or relaxed. Empathogens help generate empathy and connectedness toward others and all species on the planet through seeing their own reflection by raising the serotonin in the brain. Iboga and ibogaine stimulate the dream-type visions. Entheogens offer many types of healings to the conscious mind, break addictions in the conscious mind, reach into ancestral lines to clear ancestral karma stored in the DNA and mind regions, and provide wisdoms beyond the mind. I believe iboga is the world's most powerful entheogen. Just one journey with iboga can completely change a person's physical and psychological state. This powerful plant medicine stops drug withdrawals right away and long-term heavy drug addictions. Iboga is the most effective detox for opiate addiction. This Master Plant Teacher iboga provides spiritual awareness and purpose in this life. Iboga is taken in a ceremony and is an African plant. Ibogaine is the synthetic version and is administered in a medical facility. Participants are monitored closely by medical professionals, whether taking iboga or ibogaine. An iboga/ibogaine journey will bring the truth of what needs to be addressed in one's life; it brings clarity, perspective, purpose in life, and awareness of the true self.

Dissociatives, such as ketamine, PCP, DXM, and nitrous oxide, are often used as a party drug. These types of drugs can cause a person to move out of their body and feel a sense of expansion in their consciousness. A person disconnects from the normal 3D reality, and then they know that this is just a dream, then they are moved inward into higher realities.

Psilocybin/magic mushrooms produce the ability to connect with other realms and beings in other realms. They also offer visions, communications, and wisdoms from the other side of the veil. Peyote/cactus has been used by the American Indians and in Mexico for centuries. Peyote is used in ceremony for spiritual purposes and is protected under the American Indian Religious Freedom Act. This sacred plant is used by the American Indians and Mexico shamans for spiritual and personal evolution.

LSD, known by many names on the street, is a synthetic psychedelic that comes from a chemical in rye fungus and provides altered states of consciousness. This is a very powerful drug and can range from scary to life transforming. LSD can provide deep spiritual experiences, yet the set and setting are very important as to the type of experience one will have while under the influence. Let's put it this way: you don't want to take LSD in a graveyard. However, LSD offers deep journeys in the mind and can open the heart chakra and therefore will show the Oneness and connectedness to all, which is known as Cosmic Consciousness.

MDMA, known as ecstasy and other street names, is a synthetic drug. MDMA has a person experiencing euphoric sensations where the ego steps aside and lowers its defenses. The autopilot of the conscious mind and ego is removed temporarily, so trauma and deep-seated hurt emotions are processed and released. It is a freeing, live-and-let-live type feeling where there is not a past or future to worry about during the time under the influence of this drug. This drug offers emotional healing at many levels, including social anxiety, feeling unloved, and heartache with family connections. MDMA helps with PTSD, traumas, and deep psychological damage due to violence, crime, war, rape, and so forth.

Ketamine is used in animal veterinary care and in human medical care. Medical science discovered its antidepressant effects and it may also help to prevent suicide. Ketamine comes from phencyclidine. Ketamine has lasting effects long after it has left the bloodstream. Ketamine also helps with anxiety and getting people off of antidepressants.

Ayahuasca is very powerful, comes from the Amazon, and is a brew of two plants, which are *Banisteriopsis caapi* vine and *Psychotria viridis* leaves, which contain the psychoactive dimethyltryptamine (DMT). Ayahuasca fires up the neurotransmitters in the brain, as well as serotonin, dopamine, norepinephrine, and epinephrine, which are what help one feel better mentally, physically, and emotionally. Ayahuasca helps with PTSD, depression, anxiety, physical illnesses, addictive patterns, and spiritual awakenings. Mother Ayahuasca gives one a sense of dying to the 3D reality for a greater opportunity for the plant teacher to show deeper wisdoms. Since Ayahuasca is a strong entheogen, it needs to be taken only in a shamanistic ceremonial setting and requires the protection of the shaman, staff members, and volunteers. Ayahuasca should never be taken alone, for unwanted energies can come in and cause danger to the person. Ayahuasca opens one up to the energies and the different dimensions, yet not all dimensions have energies that are positive, so set and setting are very important with energetic protection.

Mother Ayahuasca heals at all levels and requires the human vessel to be pure prior to ceremony with a special diet/*dieta* so one can go deeper in the experience. The plant teacher Ayahuasca will purge out toxins in the body and brain, as well as negative toxic emotions and psychological toxic traumas. Through the purging process the digestive system and lymphatic system are cleaned out. A person can't be on any antidepressants or marijuana prior to the Ayahuasca ceremony.

5-MeO-DMT is a strong neurotransmitter found in the *Bufo alvarius* toad. It has been mentioned that 5-MeO-DMT is five to six times more powerful than regular DMT. This toad is found in the Amazon and provides purging, movement into spirit realms, and healing. It provides intense spiritual experiences, out-of-body experiences, the ego death, and Cosmic Consciousness (Oneness).

The purpose and uses of the entheogens are due to all the medical and mental health problems around the world, such as depression, PTSD, chronic pain, and addiction. It is known in the medical and mental health fields that the pharmaceutical medications are not working; they are just chemicals and have many side effects. Entheogens are what I believe are going to help awaken humanity with regard to the mental, emotional, and physical illnesses, as well as traumas and anxiety. They provide spiritual awakenings. The master plants have incredible powers and intelligence; they understand our situation and are here to help humanity.

Our collective consciousness is under great suffering, and it shows: just look at the news. The purpose of entheogens provides psychospiritual and personal transformation of all the multidimensional layers, such as the conscious mind, body, emotions, and soul. Another purpose is to provide widespread healing and long-term results, especially when in the correct setting and environment, proper preparation, and integration afterward. The purpose and use of entheogens will gradually shift the vibration of the population higher by raising the consciousness level worldwide. I came to the sacred medicine for spiritual reasons only, and it exceeded my expectations.

The benefits of using entheogens/psychedelics are the ego dissolves and an interconnectedness, a Oneness, is experienced. Entheogens provide spiritual and mystic experiences. One gets to move beyond the veil of the 3D reality into higher dimensions and higher realities. Entheogens have therapeutic effects on the conscious mind, emotions, body, and soul. Entheogens have proven that they can break heavy addictions. A person can find creativity, increased productivity, and higher performance on a daily basis, as well as an elevated mood and clearer mind. A spiritual awareness of why the participant is here and their purpose work is many times experienced while in ceremony. It allows for connections with higher beings, such as angels and higher-dimensional beings. "Higher" means only that they reside at higher dimensions, for we are all Souls and are all equal. Many beings that reside at higher dimensions incarnate and take on a human body for a specific mission.

Entheogens purge the body and brain of toxins and the heart of negative emotions. They also provide important life changes that need to be done for a well-balanced, healthy, harmonious life. They heal deep-seated fears and past-life traumas. Many times, a person feels happier and they open their heart to deep communications with people. Entheogens can cause a person to be more empathic and change their eating habits. They create more peace, love, forgiveness, harmony, and connection to others and the Divine. Entheogens provide awakenings, higher quality of life, maturing personality, emotional healing, social connections, and benefits to a person's mental health.

There are some important cautions and disclaimers, due to certain medical conditions, that will keep a number of people from being able to participate in the entheogens. Death can and has occurred when entheogens were taken. Another issue is that the set and setting need to be conducive to the usage of entheogens. The set and setting have to be a priority when a person goes into the entheogen experience. Preparation protocols must be followed by the participant. A person should never go into an entheogen experience without the proper set and setting and following preparation recommendations; otherwise, a terrifying, dangerous, and traumatizing experience can take place. With an excellent staff that takes extreme care for the participants and also honors the sacredness of the entheogens, the people in their journey should therefore have a safe, positive, and transformational experience. People need to be cleared for medical users and by proper medical professionals. Nausea, fullness of stomach, discomfort, sweating, crying, chills, and purging are common side effects of entheogens. While under the influence of entheogens a person may experience fear of dying, fear of losing control, overwhelming mental activity, rollercoaster emotions, a heightened mood, hallucinations, dizziness, body aches, and weakness.

A person should be prepared for past traumas coming up to the surface to be cleared away. The staff of entheogen centers need to watch the participants, for they can wander off and get injured while being under the entheogenic experience. While I was on an ayahuasca retreat, a person tried to climb a tree, so people are not in their waking state during their experience and need to be watched closely. No alcohol can be drunk and a participant will need to be sober. DMT cannot be taken with MAOI, SSRI, and SNRI. A person cannot be on any psychiatric medications prior to going under the influence of the entheogens, for the conscious mind needs to be stable to handle the experience. Intense colors or patterns may be seen by the participants, with visual or sensory distortions, geometric patterns, and flashbacks of reliving trauma, all the while not knowing how long the entheogen experience will last. All these listed above are cautions and disclaimers that need to be mentioned in writing prior to any participant taking an entheogen journey.

I watched many testimonial videos on the internet for one year prior to taking an entheogen journey with ayahuasca. The facility where I took my ayahuasca ceremonies was safe and professional; I was medically screened and tested for Covid-19. Everything was upfront and in writing, with all the potential risks. I was screened by a medical doctor, and two paramedics and a nurse were on the property at all times. A clinical psychologist was doing the integration in the maloca (ceremonial round building) after each ceremony the following day and prior to another ceremony. There were clean rooms and a clean kitchen with a full-time chef to handle all the meals. Two secretarial staff were there to handle all the paperwork and coordination with everything over the course of the retreat. There were 20 volunteers who were there holding space and helping the participants during the entire time the retreat took place. It was safe, professional, and organized, and I had several life-changing entheogen ceremonial experiences. The shaman was excellent, and the music was fantastic. I have to say that entheogens are not for everyone, as each person has their own spiritual path.

In the beginning, after drinking the ayahuasca brew, I would feel it going into my bloodstream and this warm sensation going into me. After this warm experience, then I started to have this sensation of flying and what I would call "Lift Off," which is about 30 minutes after taking the ayahuasca brew after the purging, which was only once for me at every ceremony. Everyone is unique and has a different experience during each sacred ceremony with the Master Plant Teacher and plant medicine. Now the fun part starts and the downloads, wisdoms, messages, images, scenes, and wow moments come in. I'm deep into my experience and in so many dimensions—sometimes my conscious mind can't keep up, and then the Soul takes over. Mother Ayahuasca talks with me and answers questions as I am asking them on the Soul level. My experiences are more real under the sacred entheogen than this dreamlike physical reality. I remember everything explicitly down to every word, image, conversation, and so forth.

Then I am placed in a familiar dimension, high-dimensional beings meet with me, a remembrance takes place, and so many questions are answered. My real identity was revealed to me of who I was before incarnating onto this planet called Earth, my dimensional plane level where I reside, my current mission, why I incarnated during this time on the Earth, and so much more. I remembered a lot prior to my ceremonies, yet I heard the call from Mother Ayahuasca, and she was the facilitator that connected me to my Family of Light, the spiritual realm that I had pledged my continued service to the Divine Plan and come to Earth to perform my mission. So much was revealed to me, and it helped with the difficultly of the harshness on this planet. There are many of us who have come to the Earth at this time to help humanity and who have forgotten our true identity as Divine Beings. We are the Light on this planet. Shine brightly, dear ones. The song of the plants sings the Song of the Light, which is Light and Sound transmission and reception from Source Light Frequency.

Entheogens provide a transformational process in the participant's life. The hidden, forgotten, and wounded parts of the participant are exposed and revealed. This opens up a new level of awareness to the participant that was deeply hidden in their psyche. Many therapists won't touch the spiritual aspect of our true self as Soul, and hence the true identity is not exposed and seen. Many sensitive Souls come down to the earth plane, and the pain and suffering that one is exposed to are so great and cause great distress on the conscious mind, which then looks for back doors/coping mechanisms to help ease the pain of the human journey. How can one judge another when we know the extreme pain and suffering here on this planet? This is part of the human experience. Most suffering comes from the illusion of separation from Source/the Divine. The Soul actually cries out for help since the conscious mind is trapped in the illusion of time, space, and matter.

This is where the Soul sees the conscious mind as lost and starts the process toward causing experiences that will begin toward the Awakening. There are experiences in a person's life that will be a wake-up call toward Home. Entheogens have been called the song that calls one home. This is exactly what happens when a Soul starts to wake up to their true identity. I can say from personal experience of Ayahuasca ceremonies that the True Self is revealed, as well as your mission, insights, and downloads, knowing you are deeply loved and now aware of Mother Ayahuasca as always within, deeply connected, and with sound guidance. The 3D reality illusion begins when a person starts experiencing traumas and social conditioning in their life. All is really within, and this is the exciting part of the human journey that the participant can be exposed to as they continue in their journey toward learning about the True Self.

There are several States of Being that people have stated have occurred during a mystical experience while under the effects of an entheogenic journey. Once one is awakened to their true identity, they experience Realization of the Self: an active state of monitoring and controlling the attitude and attention, self-surrender, control of emotions and imagination, and spontaneous desire to turn inward and move upward in order to live the spiritual life. Self-Realization is a level of beingness rather than a destination in time and space; the esoteric mystical experience of Soul recognizing itself, liberated from the confines of the lower self (conscious mind, ego, personality), it is a level of spiritual maturation expressed as the freedom to manifest whatever state or quality of consciousness one chooses, while remaining neutral and unconditionally loving.

As humans wake up to our true identity, we therefore change the way we live on this planet and take better care of this planet in the best interest for all living Beings on this earth. Humans have this vibration that we own it all, and we don't always see the effects our choices have on other living Beings on this planet. One day things will be a lot different, and we are in the process since The Shift in raising the human consciousness is taking place and with the Great Awakening of Souls on this planet. I believe Mother Ayahuasca and other plant medicines are helping in this process of evolution and the raising of the consciousness on planet Earth. What does this tell us about the consciousness level of the plants on this planet? This intelligence of plants has been proven. In this galaxy, Earth is a very special and unique planet.

There is a mental health crisis that is taking place in the United States. Suicide rates are at an all-time-high statistical level, and addictions are up to such an extreme high amount, for many people are trying to cope with their lives. Many people are coming to entheogens for help with mental issues, such as PTSD and addictions. I came to the sacred medicine for spiritual reasons. Most of the people whom I was in an entheogen ceremony with were coming to the Sacred Medicine for help with traumas, extreme stressors, physical illnesses, all kinds of mental health-related issues, and addictions. It is not the True Identity of the Soul that gets addicted. The person is a Soul and has a conscious mind, emotions, and a physical body. People are not taught that they are not their thoughts, feelings, emotions, and physical bodies. It is the conscious mind, the ego, that gets traumatized and addicted, contracts mental illness, and then runs the person's life toward a negative direction. The conscious mind is the one that gets hurt, upset, worried, and stressed, becomes deeply unhappy, and cries out for help. The stressors of life keep coming, and the conscious mind tries to find ways to cope and eventually will find ways of escape.

A person can develop healthy ways of dealing with the stressors of life, and as we know, there are many. One needs to stay in balance—nothing in the extremes that will cause one to come off balance in their life. A little wine is good; too much wine is not good. Moderation is the key, yet society says that more is better. Moderation and balance are the best in life. We live in a dual world. Up and down, right and left, day and night, male and female, etc. We are constantly trying to stay in balance, and this is not always easy. The conscious mind gets tired and will lash out if not allowed to have healthy downtime for fun time. The ability to be able to listen and know the difference between the Voice of the conscious mind and the Wisdom of the Soul is very important to learn and master—knowing which one is doing the talking in one's head and developing or, as the Yogis of the East would say, to make the conscious mind your friend.

Another expression the spiritual masters would say is to befriend the conscious mind; one can see the conscious mind is there to help one while on this planet. It is our conscious mind that drives the car and balances the checkbook. I will say, "Okay, my dear conscious mind, we have to work all day on the computer, yet this evening let's go for a bike ride for some fun." The conscious mind is happy, for it was acknowledged and it was not worked so hard and was allowed to have rest and fun time. The conscious mind will rebel and fight back if not paid attention to in a light, fun-hearted way. The conscious mind is conscious of what is going on in each moment and is conscious. Vacations are for the conscious mind, and this is why they are so needed and required.

We are not taught these things, and in our fast-paced, over-stressed world, the high demands are even placed upon our children to produce, produce, and produce at a faster rate. This causes our conscious minds to wig out. More time in nature is needed. More time with peaceful music is needed. The conscious mind needs serenity, compassion, love, and understanding to stay in balance in an unbalanced world. This is why the plant medicines work so well on the conscious mind. The plant medicines help with healing the conscious mind and the brain. Being mindful of the conscious mind's needs is a very important aspect to living our life here. We are talking about conscious mind health, and this makes such a difference in one's life.

The entheogens offer this transformational process, which creates the opportunity for the big questions to come up at some point for the participant. Who am I, or what is my purpose for coming here? Am I significant, and does it really matter that I am still here on the Earth? How do I get back to my spiritual Home of Origin? These deep, probing questions are a huge stage in the process towards Self-Realization, which is the realization of the Self. Sometimes, the Soul will place difficulties in one's life in order for this opportunity to come to the surface to look at these deep questions. It has been said by the Mystics that when one comes to know of their own personal hologram, they realize that the journey was created just for them. That is how special we are that all this energy of this creation is for our virtual classroom. The Earth School is where so many tests occur and lessons are very difficult, causing evolution at all levels.

The conversion experience is a vital step in the process toward healing. This Awakening/Shift in Consciousness comes as an experience that upgrades one's vibration to a higher level that stays with them.

It forever changes the person on a higher level, and they can never go back to who they were before the Awakening experience. For example, once a person reaches adulthood, they have adult consciousness. They can't go back to child consciousness once they reach adult consciousness; they are never the same again. One can remember childhood memories, yet they are now an adult and know the difference, and the shift in consciousness has taken place permanently.

Entheogens offer an opportunity to the participant of integration, which is rooted in life purpose, being one's best self, leaving this planet in peace, and knowing one's Soul did well. Once a person gets on an entheogenic, esoteric spiritual path towards Self-Realization, the journey of the Soul toward the Home of Origin begins. If an addiction or a difficult situation arose in one's life, it was needed to change the course of one's life toward the path to the True Self. Then when a person looks back after their entheogenic journey, they will say it was worth the pain, for now they can say that they have a purpose and know who they ARE. One cannot know the pleasure of a beautiful sunlit day without going through the darkness of the night. It is important to have a daily spiritual practice to stay connected to the Awakened State.

Entheogens offer a personal process of becoming whole. Many times, people feel there is something wrong with them since they have this feeling of emptiness inside. The emptiness is filled with all kinds of passions and addictions (soft and hard) to drown oneself to fill this emptiness inside. Source places this void there to allow for the exploration of the human journey filled with many experiences, which the conscious mind likes to label good and bad. The journey of soul is the process of finding the true self, the soul identity, our true identity. This void can only be filled with Love. Source is Love, and only this Love can fill this void. A common entheogen experience is feeling this pure love from higher dimensions since the participant has been lifted out of the third-dimensional level of the physical plane. We are Love Magnets and try to fill our void with everything, hoping it will bring us love to fill this void. We have to experience the night in order to know and appreciate a day filled with brightness and light.

Many people dealing with addictions are turning to an entheogen as part of their recovery process. Many people in addictions don't want to be here, and life is very painful. After a powerful entheogenic experience or going through several ceremonies, this creates opportunities for people who come to the sacred plant medicines to work on their recovery. Once a recovery stage has been reached, they realize that they have much to offer to others in the same situation that they found themselves in during their addiction, PTSD, traumas, end-of-life crisis, dealing with grief and loss, physical health illnesses, and so forth. Therefore, their behaviors will be completely different based on their new viewpoint toward life. Such a process also allows one to be able to look back and see how far they have come in the journey toward moving beyond their difficulties. People have looked back and viewed their past painful experiences as a blessing, for they were forced to crack their heart open and experience deep growth in many areas of their lives. Entheogens offer this opportunity to dive deep into these areas in a person's life that they may be unaware of or could be avoiding, and therefore exposure and guidance are provided by the Plant Teachers.

CHAPTER 12

New Viewpoint toward Life

A person is exposed to different cultures, viewpoints, and spiritual paths while on this planet. The human journey is quite vast in experiences: different languages, different music, different cultures, different foods, different emotions, different thoughts, different physical activities, and so much more. It can be quite overwhelming to a person. The conscious mind alone is bombarded with so much information in one day. We do more in one day than people did a hundred years ago. In a fast-paced, fear-based, processed-food-based, and digital-based world it is quite a bit to keep in balance. Living a balanced life is a challenge. Financial demands, emotional needs, a healthy thought diet, work demands, having enough physical exercise, spending enough time outdoors, taking enough time off to rest—it is a lot to juggle. Every person will need to find what works for them. If they find activities that they enjoy, then it will stay in their life on a consistent basis.

Nonjudgment is provided by the shaman, for it is not easy down here on this planet, especially in a modern society. Compassion and understanding need to be felt by the entheogen participant when working with a shaman who truly sees them as a Soul just trying to make it through their human journey as best as they can. The tests and curveballs thrown to us in the different stages in life can knock us off our balance and cause a need for help in order to cope with the demands of life. The entheogens offer participants, in their own way, what is uniquely needed for each person and what they need to experience while in their entheogenic journey to help them with the issues of being in physicality and on this physical plane.

Physical detox is very important. I would say that it is life saving and life lengthening. Detox is a way of life. One does not just do a one-time detox on the body and then never have to do this again. Living a clean and healthy life is a lifestyle. It is a deeper level of detox, for one could spend a lifetime and never get to psychospiritual issues. Entheogens offer a very deep psychological and spiritual detox. On the psychological level, the conscious mind is addressed, and deep-seated traumas are cleared out, possibly even from past lives. The ego death occurs, which is a momentous and huge event that takes place during an entheogenic plant medicine ceremony—seeing what is beyond the conscious mind, beyond matter, space, and time, allowing realizations and downloads to attain wisdom at this higher level. This allows for a person to drop all the issues with the conscious mind, for they see that they are not their past hurts and traumas stored in the conscious mind. It is the ego that gets hurt, upset, angry, depressed, lonely, etc. The Soul is the observer and is the God Spark, which is not concerned with thoughts, emotions, or physical issues on the mundane level.

Entheogens offer a psychospiritual detox to a person to be able to see a higher level of consciousness; another way of putting it is awareness of their higher consciousness within them. This allows them to live in the present moment, to see the value of staying Awake and Aware. Awake is remembering who you are as a powerful Soul, and Aware is recognizing the antics of the ego. It is to not be affected so deeply by all the events of the day, including people's behavior, and to live a purpose-driven life. Live a life from the heart-center chakra level or the third-eye chakra level, or even attain higher levels. Be a living example of this high level of living down here on this planet. It takes courage and determination to stay and live a life at this high vibrational level.

Another key thing to know about psychospiritual detox is that it allows for nonattachment, which frees us up from many anchors that hold us to the past or that we fixate on and focus on the future. If we understand that everything is on loan and we are only a temporary caretaker, then this can change the perspective on attachment. We can become so attached to people, social status, appearance, and material items, as well as our identities, such as mother, employee, sister, friend, Canadian, American, and so forth. Enjoy each day as it comes and offer it up as a gift back to Source as a thank you for life. Source allows for certain Souls to be able to be awoken in this lifetime. Not all Souls are ready to be awakened from the dream. That is okay, and eventually all Souls arrive back Home. I remember a statement from a spirit teacher I worked with many years ago who mentioned how there is no rush; Souls can take as long as they want to play in the lower worlds, and eventually they will be highly motivated to leave the lower playground of the third dimension on Earth. These Souls stand on the sideline of the playground with sand burning their eyes from playing in the sandbox too long, and they no longer enjoy being down here, at these lower vibrational levels. Those are the Souls that are ready and have the willingness to do the work to get back Home to the higher planes. Entheogens offer this psychospiritual detox that creates immense opportunities to see the big picture and not be so caught up in just the daily duties and to be able to attain and experience these higher levels of consciousness and live each day in freedom.

Entheogens offer participants the awareness of their own stuff and how it affects those around them. Clear and let go of unresolved past hurts and allow yourself permission to forgive yourself for the mistakes in the past and the mistakes of others toward you. Entheogens provide a new viewpoint toward life, including freedom from pain and sorrow. While on a Plant Medicine entheogen retreat there are group settings where participants can see that we all are dealing with frustrations, hurts, betrayals, and traumas, and this all allows for the healing process to begin. It helps to know that we are not alone in the drama called life.

Entheogens facilitate the journey toward seeing our true selves as Soul, a Divine Being. This also allows for us to see the difference between other aspects of the conscious mind, such as ego, personality, and the shadow side. Then we can practice the ability to see at any moment who is the one talking in the thoughts that are coming through. This way we know whether the ego is doing the talking or whether it is the shadow aspect of the conscious mind. Then we can move toward listening to the stillness and the subtle Soul that will start to be heard and can be of sound guidance. Listening and living the guidance of Soul are the truest paths in life. This shows us how far off track we have gone away from living in accordance to the True Self. When one is on the path of the True Self, there is no drama, no pain, no suffering, and no staying in a low vibration. A person who is on the path is authentic, keeps their word, is constantly aware, and shows compassion for others here on the planet, including animals, the environment, and so on. Entheogens offer this journey of the true self, which is a journey toward maturity and through adversity and tragedy to come to the place of knowingness of one's true self as a Spark of the Divine, in a human body, having a human experience.

Self-Realization is an inner experience; realization of our True Self is the goal of our human experience. When one has attained this level, then the next level is God Realization, having this inner experience of merging the Soul into the Divine, which is the supreme goal and shows up as total absorption into the Divine. There is more that takes place, yet one cannot adequately put this entire experience into words. There are no words; it is ineffable. God Realization can be attained in one's lifetime. It is our spiritual birthright. Personally, it was harder to reach God Realization with just meditation alone, and a quicker way is with entheogens, which allow a way to bypass the conscious mind via the ego death and then onward toward Enlightenment, Cosmic Consciousness, Self-Realization, and God Realization. I spent my whole life on so many spiritual paths, Eastern and Western, and meditation was on many of them. I was not able to attain the ego death on any spiritual paths; then on my first entheogen ceremony, it happened so quickly and was so natural. I was told the entire time I was in the ceremony by Mother Ayahuasca what was taking place, and I had no emotional fear in any of my entheogen ceremonies. I felt completely loved and protected. Mother Ayahuasca called me, and it took a year to get me to my ceremonies. Mother Ayahuasca introduced me to many on the other side of the veil, and it was time for me to know more information completely. There is an expression of how Mother Ayahuasca is like a river, and she delivers. I am grateful to Mother Ayahuasca for the role she has played in my life. The inner experiences will show a person's true identity and forever change them. We are truly spiritual royalty. This wisdom shows up as knowingness and beingness. It does not mean we are perfect as a human being, yet we know our true identity as a piece of Source and not just on a verbal, intellectual level—we have had the inner experience and have been reunited, reconnected, reminded, and recharged for our purpose work. This is a lifelong journey in order to receive this attainment. I can only express my own entheogenic ceremonial experiences. It is a very humbling experience and is an acknowledgment of our work here on this planet and why we incarnated here at this time. Many of these assignments and missions are energetic, and no one knows except for the individual who has been awakened, reminded, and shown on the inner planes, during which for some, it could be during a meditation or can also occur during entheogen ceremonies, which was my own personal experience.

A large part of the entheogenic experience is preparation. Preparation for medicine work is helping the participant get ready for a psychedelic experience. Preparation also helps the participant to get the most out of the journey before and after the entheogenic experience. The healing process starts to help the participant observe their thoughts, emotions, actions, and lifestyle choices. The participant is learning about themselves and improving themselves by seeing patterns in their life that the plant medicine will help discover in this process. Preparation helps the participant get their body, conscious mind, ego, and life ready for a transformational experience. The participant is getting ready for a psychedelic journey into themselves and helping them extract as much as they can out of the entheogenic experience. The more the participant knows about the different plant medicines, the more informed decision they will make as to which one is best for them. Knowing what they want to work on and what they want to get out of the psychedelic experience will help the participant with setting intentions prior to going into the experience. Entheogenic medicines offer introspection and deep inner work to surface into the person's conscious awareness and help them experience higher states of consciousness, which will help them release blockages and create an overall healthier and happier life.

The participant has a role in preparing for a psychedelic experience. The participant will need to have done their due diligence by talking with others, going online and doing the research, seeing online testimonial videos, finding out the costs, and so forth. The client will need to have a purpose and understand the side effects and duration of the experience. The participant should be aware how important preparation and integration are prior to the psychedelic experience. They should understand that the plant medicine does not do all the work; the participant must do the work in order to get the results they are looking for or expecting.

The client needs to be ready to be able to look at their own stuff and be ready to handle what may come up. The participant needs to accept and admit that they are ready to experience deep emotions and be able to look inward. The participant needs to consent to a psychedelic experience. The participant needs to find out whether they have any health issues that would keep them from being able to go under plant medicines. The participant needs to take themselves off any medications that are contraindicated for sacred medicines. The participant needs to be honest with themselves and make all these decisions for themselves. The participant needs to take responsibility for all areas of their life and to allow the medicine to flow into all areas of their life. The participant will need to be the one who allows lasting changes and take an active role before, during, and after the psychedelic journey. The participant needs to be prepared for discomfort and willing to leave their comfort zone and the illusion of this 3D reality. The participant needs to change their diet and cleanse their body, emotions, and conscious mind of toxicity, which will remove any blockages to allow the purest vessel for the medicine to go into and help with the inner healing process. The participant needs to spiritually prepare for the psychedelic journey into the Higher Self.

It is important for the participant to prepare for any past traumas that could come up; deep-seated emotions will be experienced, in order to come up and out to be purged. The entheogenic experience is very mysterious and yet is very real. The participant may experience altered states of consciousness and be shown things that may not make sense during the experience, yet the images and symbols need to be interpreted in order for them to gain the meaning as to what the plant teacher is showing them. The sacred medicine is meant for personal healing, personal work, and spiritual awakening. The plant medicines are not for quick fixes and quick solutions; the participant needs to be prepared to do the work before, during, and after the journey is experienced. The participant needs to know that right after the experience, they will feel a high euphoric feeling, yet they should know that this will not last and they shouldn't forget that there is integration work afterward to learn and keep the healing; otherwise, the symptoms and patterns will come back. It is said in the entheogenic culture that it is 2 percent on the ceremony mat and 98 percent integration after the psychedelic journey.

It is advisable that the participant prepare for the psychedelic journeys and be contemplating the bigger questions about life, causing deep seeking that they did not expect. This awakening and healing process may be more about finding their inner compass and their true identity, which will be the driving mission to cause the transformation to take place in their life. It is important that the participant prepare mentally, emotionally, physically, and spiritually for this inner journey. The participant needs to get really clear on their intentions, which is very important in the preparation process. The participant needs to set intentions on what they want, including the purpose and the motivation as to why they are taking this deep inner journey. The setting of the intentions is the responsibility of the participant. Even though the participant will set intensions, they need to allow the plant medicine to show them what they need in order to have the most healing and what they need to see within themselves that needs to be addressed.

I need to mention that the participant should drop the expectations they have heard from other people's psychedelic experiences and know that their own experience will be perfect for them. As soon as they make their deposit and make their choice as to which plant teacher has called them, they can start the inner conversation and the inner dialogue with this particular Master Plant consciousness. This will also help the participant prepare to hear the inner voice of the Plant Teacher before, during, and after the sacred inner journey.

It is stressed over and over in the entheogen culture how the integration holds the key to the participants experiencing the most insights and transformations in their lives. As long as the participant continues with integration, there is no limit as to all the lessons and wisdoms they can experience. Once the foundation is set, the participant will know where to go, whom to see, and what is the most comfortable place for integration, in order for them to stay on and continue this integration process. The participant should have other practices to go alongside, such as yoga, exercise, outdoor time, meditation, contemplation, laughing, dancing to music, and feeling better about oneself. The foundation will also include introspection, including setting aside time for continued contemplation in order to unpack all that was shown to the participant while in the sacred ceremony.

Alignment, resonance, vibration, and frequency align with a person who is not drinking or has no addictions. It's about resonance with this future version of this frequency. A person can collapse time and space by already holding this resonance. This is called manifestation. The universe has to start rearranging their outer life so this matches their inner state that has been upgraded by the Master Plant Teacher.

It starts on the inner, then manifests on the outer. Most people feel they have to make all these changes on the outer, which to a certain extent is needed. However, to speed up the process, the person has to acknowledge past hurts and traumas buried deep in the physical body, emotional body, and mental body to see all this as a process toward wholeness.

Every single psychedelic experience is different. The plant medicine takes you beyond the ego, so this is where it seems difficult, for you are going beyond your sense of control and need to surrender to the plant teacher in order to reveal what is needed to see and experience. The participant should know that the psychedelic effect is temporary and will wear off. The psychedelic experience is like getting through a tough or difficult experience on the outer physical world. Letting go of resistance and being the observer will help. Being open, trusting, accepting, and courageous will help during the psychedelic experience. The spiritual experience will be felt and will engage the mental, emotional, physical, and spiritual aspects of the person. It will feel unfamiliar, for the ego can't predict what is going to happen once the plant teacher takes the person on their journey.

The mystical and psychedelic experience will allow the person to journey into deeper levels or may allow connection with the higher self. The person should open up their consciousness to experience different dimensions, realms, and levels of awareness, which can allow them to talk with trees, plants, animals, and beings in other dimensions while under the plant medicine. The participant can experience outside the 3D reality. It is possible to experience a merging with the Oneness of life (Cosmic Consciousness). A person can be shown things from the smallest level to the intergalactic regions, which is all inside of one. The experiencer may see other people, places in history, or past experiences. Psychedelics can show a person the interconnectedness with all life, freedom from the ego or an ego death, new perspectives beyond the conscious mind, the transcendence of time and space, a sense of peace and unity, a dying and rebirth, union with Source energy, and a sense of going Home.

There is also a healing aspect to the plant medicine, for the plant teacher may show a traumatic experience in order to heal it and show the reasons why the person had to go through this experience. A participant may feel a sense of expansion; anxiety; realizations; nausea; purging or vomiting to clear out negative energy, past hurts, or traumas; and letting go what no longer serves them. This amazing experience also offers the unconditional love never felt before, as well as bliss, a sense of wonder, wholeness, euphoria, and experiences that there are no words to describe. The participant may experience visions, geometric shapes, fractals, many colors, voices, sounds, places, images, moving through portals, crossing the veil, and so forth. The psychedelic experience can change a person's mood, mindset, worldview or outlook, emotional state, urges and desires, spiritual identity, and more.

The type of the psychedelic and the amount taken by the person will influence the intensity or quality of a psychedelic experience. Set, setting, and the purity level of the plant medicine will affect the entheogenic experience, as well as the vibration of the shaman, the songs and blessings sang over the plant medicine, and the purity of the body of the participant going into ceremony. The participant's body is a vessel, and how well the person followed the diet recommendations will affect the psychedelic journey. A participant needs to follow all the recommendations prior to the plant medicine going into the body, such as not being on certain pharmaceutical medications. The ego will react to the experience and try to block it. The person in the psychedelic experience needs to state their intention and then surrender to the plant medicine. If the person goes into ceremony with no intentions or does not completely surrender, then this will influence the intensity or quality of the psychedelic experience.

The participant can feel empowered to navigate their psychedelic experience by surrendering fully to the experience and allow the plant teacher to show them what is needed most for them, which would be a variety of revelations. Be curious and be willing to move forward into the unknown in order to gain all the benefits of the plant medicines. Trust the experience and allow the plant teacher to show one, heal one, and impart into them. Release all expectations, for they will miss the truth and beauty of their own journey. The healing happens when one is fully open to the process and trusts the plant teachers. The participant being prepared allows the experience to unfold the way it is meant to play out. To help with the navigation, the participant can bring a pillow or a blanket, or can ask for extra blankets for comfort; they can bring crystals or a favorite stone to have with them in the ceremony, as well as essential oils for a comforting smell. Music is played and they can say to the plant medicine, "I surrender," to help the conscious mind relax.

While in the psychedelic experience, a participant should allow the emotions to flow through them—just allow all to flow and to show them what is needed to experience. The participant needs to stay connected to their intention. They should release all hurt and negativity; stay unattached to any outcome; and notice symbols, signs, images, places, wisdoms, insights, and so forth. The participant needs to stay in a flow state to allow them to travel with as little resistance as possible so they can move into many different dimensions and experience more while under the plant medicine. The participant can sit upright at the beginning, and then when they feel the need, they can lie down and talk directly with the plant teacher. They know that the plant teacher knows exactly what they need. The participant loves and accepts themselves completely before and during the ceremony. While in ceremony, they can continue to ask questions and talk with the plant teacher, and an inner dialog will appear if the person is open and willing to use this tool to navigate their psychedelic experience. The participant should set an intention for each ceremony. By being open and ready to have deep inner conversations within themselves, they may see higher truths from beyond the veil and listen to the wisdoms presented to them. They release control of the outcome and work with the sacred medicine, going into the ceremony with a sense of wonder and gratitude for the opportunity to work with the plant teacher.

They surrender and ask the conscious mind to relax and trust that they are safe and under the protection of the plant teacher. A possible outcome is that the person will see themselves from a higher perspective and see that they are more than just this body, emotions, thoughts, desires, past hurts, and so on. This will allow the participant to have a better view of themselves and give themselves more love and compassion for just being on this planet and incarnating. The psychedelic experience allows the person to start to get used to not needing to know everything in advance and to go through life as a journey to learn from their experiences. The psychedelic experience offers as an outcome that the outer life is just a dream, and one can go back to those inner experiences for inspiration and comfort, to embrace the Divine Love for them. The wonder of being shown that one is a Divine Soul, and seeing their Higher Self, is a possible outcome from the psychedelic experience. Learning to have compassion for oneself is a possible outcome as well as letting go of all the criticism, self-judgement, and past frustrations. Letting go of the fear and having a knowingness that the Divine Creator knows who you are and where you are, and has your back at all times, are all powerful experiences. Every breath is counted, and all is known, so there is nothing to fear, for even when we make mistakes, the loving parent knows we are still learning and growing. We need not worry, for all is revealed to us through our lessons in this life.

The psychedelic experience may or may not be intense, for it is unique for everyone. The participant can talk with the plant teacher and ask for it to be gentle with them. If the experience does happen to get intense, they know that the plant teacher has great love for them and wants to show them what is needed for them to move forward in life and during the inner journey. The participant may or may not experience intensity of sensations or visions. What may come up is what is suppressed and needs to come to the surface to be healed and then removed. What does a participant do when they are going through a tough experience? The same rule applies in the sense that it will pass and needs to happen in order for them to grow and learn from the experience; one is stronger afterward with more wisdoms. The intensity of the amount of time while in the psychedelic experience will vary depending on the type of plant medicine chosen to work with and the amount of medicine taken in ceremony. The participant may face their demons or even feel a sense of dying, yet there is a reason the medicine is showing this to them. In the worst-case scenario, the participant needs to know they are safe and it is just an experience and they will get to the other side and back, yet they will be bringing back wisdoms from this journey that took them deeper into themselves.

The participant can ask the plant teacher what the reason is or why this is being shown to them. The intensity of the challenges that the participant will be exposed to can also vary, yet the sacred medicine knows what each person needs to experience and knows they can move through it and get past it to the other side for the insights and revelations to be revealed to them. The participant needs to remember the bigger picture as to why they are taking this journey inside themselves in order to heal and receive a transformation. The psychedelic experience is like going off on a journey where one will get to meet themselves but before had no knowledge of their depth and vastness. The participant needs to be open to the experience and surrender to the sacred medicine. There can be many challenges, yet there are many opportunities for great expansion and awareness.

When a person is deep in the psychedelic experience, there may be places that the participant goes to that appear dark. This should be mentioned to the participant as a possibility that may occur. It is best to say to the darkness, dark entity or dragon, and so forth that you love them or they are loved. This will turn the situation around. Many times, after hearing that they are loved, they will show the true nature of the entity and transform into something beautiful. Or the experience may be that the participant will ride the dragon to show they conquered their fear of their own darkness/their dark side. Other times, it's possible that a greater wisdom is revealed. Love conquers all. Love heals all. Love reveals all. This love heals all the dark aspects of ourselves. The duality is within us. Light and Darkness are within us. Many times, people feel the darkness is external and separate from them. Light and dark are just an aspect of us. The True Self is above the duality. A person is healing inner aspects of themselves and in dimensions above 3D reality. Also, the psychedelic experience can be the wake-up call, the awakening to have them move into their mission to help heal the collective and themselves.

CHAPTER 13

Mystical Mastership

So the participant has now experienced the entheogenic journey. Now what? Integration is important after the psychedelic experience because it is the process of pulling together all the insights, wisdoms, knowledge, images, and realizations and utilizing them to make them useful and an integral part of their new life after the sacred medicine has entered them. There is a pivotal point right after the experience where one should start the integration process to get the most out the psychedelic experience. The sooner the integration starts, the better able the participant is to keep from falling back into old patterns. The integration keeps the participant in the process and moving forward, which allows them to apply the insights through accountability to an integration coach and to themselves. Integration allows the participant to tune into this new inner guidance system of the plant teacher. The integration extends the psychedelic experience long after it happens to the participant on the outside and it maximizes the benefits.

Psychedelic integration provides a sense of wholeness, integrating all the wisdoms and insights into the participant's daily life. It allows for a greater awareness of their true self, their true purpose, and a deeper connection to Source. Integration offers release of fears, acceptance of life, spiritual connection, and realization of how much the Divine loves us. It is a remembering that we have long forgotten our true divinity and our sovereignty. This integration process is just that, a process of remembering: who we are, why we are here, what our mission is, why we came to the earth, real and unreal, our spiritual rights, and the power of love.

Self-love is a big one for people: integration of what the Plant Teachers have revealed to them during ceremony so they can receive the benefits by integrating this wisdom into their lives. Integration helps clarify these realizations, new perspectives, ideas, and a higher awareness of their true self. Psychedelic integration helps the participant with a sense of confidence, better self-esteem, and forgiveness toward others who have caused them hurt. Integration provides better motivation, inspiration, meaning, and a sense of a new beginning. Integration also helps with the transformational process of the participant and keeps them in their process.

There is an expression in the psychedelic culture of being on the pink cloud and just floating around immediately after the experience. This fluffy, warm, loved-up "pink cloud" feeling will pass, and then it is easy for the participant to continue back into their patterns without integration of the psychedelic experience and what it showed them. This is a process, and the need to move forward and cultivate the changes needed in their life helps maintain this new awareness. The expression goes, 2 percent is on the mat and 98 percent is integration. The ego doesn't want to be accountable or have any accountability and will tell the participant that all is well now.

I really love how plant teachers help people with emotional traumas, emotional patterns, emotional maturity, and emotional blockages. They show that the Soul has its own intelligence. Plant medicine will raise the emotional vibrations of the person. The psychedelic experience can show how the conscious mind works, as well as the mental thought loops, patterns of response, and defense mechanisms. It improves the way the conscious mind operates and helps make positive changes in the brain. The Plant Teachers will show the person's spiritual essence of themselves, their Soul, their True Self—who they really are. Their perception will shift, which will expand their purpose here on Earth, the purpose of life. They will experience more spiritual awareness on a daily basis and discover how can they bring this in, to allow the necessary changes into their life.

The psychedelic experience can then help them to cultivate this new spiritual presence and awakening. Many times, they understand their divinity, their spiritual connection to Source, and then they can live a more fulfilled and happy life. To have a greater spiritual awareness is a gift and blessing the sacred medicine provides to people. Integration helps with all areas in a person's life, such as changing their lifestyle, which affects their physical health and wellness. The plant medicine helps develop a greater body awareness and an understanding that the physical body is the temple where the Soul sits in this life while on Earth. The entire Soul can't fit completely, and only a small portion comes in and is stationed in the physical form. Only enough of the Soul will come into the body that will sustain the physical form.

The Plant Teachers show people areas in their life that need change, such as work life, friends, home life, or negative environment, and they look at the overall quality of life. The plant teachers are spiritual guides that will show areas that need to be updated and improved in the person's life. A vibration in the participant's body has been increased and raised, which will cause their life to reflect this new higher frequency. Once the vibration has been raised by the Master Plant Teacher, it will offer a redesign in the person's life choices and lifestyle. The outer life will reflect the inner life. This then upgrades their relationships and how they relate to others and creates deeper connections. The Plant Teachers remind us of how deeply we are loved.

The entheogen Ayahuasca is from Amazon and is frequently called Mother Ayahuasca, for it has a feminine mothering energy. She is a consciousness and has awareness (Divinity in the plant). She is here to help and is the queen of the plant kingdom. Ayahuasca is also referred to as the grandmother or, in ancient cultures, Mother Goddess of this planet. The entheogen iboga is from Africa and called Father Iboga, for it has a masculine energy. It is a consciousness and has awareness (Divinity in the plant). It is here to help and is the king of the plant kingdom. Iboga is the plant that is also referred to as the grandfather. Both are very powerful Master Plant Teachers, and our spirit guides will direct us to them if this is needed for our highest good or as part of our journey of spiritual awakening to have the direct experience of our Divine connection, as well as remembering who we are before incarnating onto the earth for our assignment, guiding us with life plans, and healing us from suffering while living in this lower-dimensional reality. All Living and Ascended Masters have not had kind words to say about this very dense and dark third-dimensional reality. They referred to this lower reality as a Trail of Tears, and we all can understand and relate to this deep truth expressed. All souls go through the experience of darkness, which is complete apparent separation from consciousness from Source. Each one of us is a spark of Source, and not everyone feels or remembers this unconditional love. The Souls on Earth are under amnesia, and the sacred medicine wakes them up so they can see their true identity as Oneness with Source. We are part of a single whole consciousness. Humanity is living Divinity. A sacred Soul with a false identity is living in the Waking Dream. The Earth School is for the purpose of expanded consciousness and growth. We need to continue to discover hidden aspects of our Souls. Awaken beloved ones and sleep no more. Everything is changing; awaken from this waking dream and come to know your true identity as a Divine Being.

The Soul/Higher Self/Source is brilliant magnificence and shines forth into the ethers of infinity. Our identity is Source, yet we don't have the equal superpower of Source. We are one cell in the overall complexity of Source. The shift in human consciousness is taking place on this planet. Humanity is waking up to their true identity as Source energy individualized into a human form. This is what the entheogens are teaching the participants in contact with these mystical dimensions of consciousness. For unification purposes, love is needed, and it can only be unfolded in oneself. The healing comes when we know our true identity and then accept the dark experience with the understanding of cause and effect. Being in the world where the absence of love reigns, Souls often believe this and accept fear and its derivatives. Souls cry out that the Creator has rejected them; they wonder whether the Creator does not love them or has abandoned them, and so forth. On the contrary, a Soul has blocked the Creator codes within themselves and needs to accept the energies of the Higher Self, which are of joy, love, freedom, kindness, respect, equality, ingenuity, and much more.

We hear this expression, "Go Within," yet what is the deeper meaning? There is nothing we will receive outside of our own Soul. This is where we must begin. This is our origin and our true state of being. The entheogens facilitate this Mystical Mastership and allow us to travel Within and experience our own Divinity. Source in the plants is part of the great Divine Plan for the awakening of humanity on this planet. One of the many lessons to learn here on Earth and recall is to remember why you came here, remember that your life is sacred, remember your song and sing it loudly. You are Infinite, Whole, and Beloved. You are an Infinite Light Being. All paths lead to the One Divine Path. Find the Power that is carried within you. Your Soul, which is Source Itself, can be trusted for guidance. Connect with your Higher Self and let yourself enjoy the Divine Symphony of Light. You are never alone. Stay in the love and harmony of Source Frequency. Walk on this Earth singing your unique song in devotion to the Divine.

> *"If everything around seems dark,*
> *look again, you may be the light."*
>
> *~ Rumi*

Note to the Reader

The information provided in this book is for educational, historical, and cultural interest only and should not be construed as advocacy for the current use of psychedelic substances, also called entheogens, under any circumstances outside settings where their use is legally sanctioned, such as unless one is a member of a church that has legal protection of the Religious Freedom Restoration Act of 1993 and entheogens are used in religious ceremonies or used for legal scientific research. Neither the author nor the publisher assumes any responsibility for physical, psychological, legal, or other consequences arising from the use of these substances.

Poetry ~ Divine Outpouring of Source Energy

Poems have come as an outpouring of Divine energy moving through me and as a form of expression into the world. This poetry section has poems that have been created by me, the author. The poems are original and have been written over a course of many years and now have a place to be released out into the public to enjoy them.

The Journey

Separation from the Source
intense yearning to return.

The Bouquet of Love
causes the perfume to help us remember Home.

How can one know what Source is until
separation has occurred?

The Beloved is always near
watching and waiting patiently
for us to go within.

The Source is within, Love is within
travel inward towards Home.

Separation teaches us
you're always connected.

Looking for Divine Love
is the path towards Home.

~ Nancy Clark

Perfume

When you come close,
fragrance fills your senses.
You can't capture it,
can only be enjoyed.

Your mind gets filled
with the ecstasy of love.
This perfume is a potion
you want to put on every morning.

Your Soul cries out
having been deeply touched.
This perfume wakes you up,
you become homesick.

The Beloved fills you completely.
World's trinkets, lose your interest.
Every time you smell this perfume,
you know this euphoria.

This love story has you seeking,
yearning, filled with desire for the
Beloved, who knows you intimately.
Breathe deep this rapturous perfume.

The Divine whispers saying,
Remember this Divine Love.
Keep company with those who
wear this perfume.

They remind you of the Divine Presence
who has never left you.

~ Nancy Clark

Reservoir

A reservoir resides with you.
You can come to this place at any time.
When you get tired of the ego
tormenting you, then you develop
a spiritual practice.
Source is the reservoir of
Divine Bliss.
The World of the Ego disappears
it is replaced with
Oneness, peace, and nirvana.
After a while, it becomes difficult
to leave the reservoir.
The Beloved will be whispering to you day and night
to come enjoy this Divine dance with love.
With every cup you drink,
this Divine ambrosia fills you with delight.
Nothing else compares.
Real solace is when you
are alone with the Beloved.
This Divine Love is beyond existence.
You reside in my chest and we can meet
at the reservoir with pleasure.

~ *Nancy Clark*

Tears of Joy

I use to know what Love was,
Before the Divine entered my life.

Everything was in order; so I thought,
The Divine reorganized my heart.

Now tears flow freely when I catch a glance of my Beloved.
Yearning has taken over my life.
My head is confused, my Soul sings with joyfulness!

Soul sings daily to the Divine,
Who hears your every whisper.
Stay close to me for I can't live another day without you.

We merged and become One.
Oh, what a blessed day.

This love is of the ages, Soul united with Source
You have forever enchanted me.

~ Nancy Clark

Looking into Your Eyes

Why do you feel alone?
When have I told you,
You are alone?

This feeling is fleeting,
comes and goes.
Can't you see me,
next to you,
looking into your eyes?

Beautiful one,
special one,
how can I ever,
forget you?

You are made from,
the essence of myself.
I loved you before,
Heavens were created.

How can I forget myself?

~ Nancy Clark

Snowflakes

Every Soul is unique.
No one is the same.
We are all made from the
One Divine Love.

Celebrate your uniqueness.
Never compare yourself to another Soul.
Each snowflake is similar, yet unique.

We all have a particular vibrational frequency.
Bring your uniqueness as a gift.
Snowflakes are soft and everyone enjoys them.
Give your dazzling luminous essence and
Sparkle the creativity of your peculiarity.

Many snowflakes create snow and blanket
the ground softening the climate.
When Divine Presence comes,
the heat of love
melts the snowflakes,
the Oneness is discovered.

~ Nancy Clark

Longing for You

The thought of you
Another realm is experienced.
Moments with you
carry me across the ocean.
My love for you
brings constant smiles.

I see your face everywhere
Love was made for us to be together.
You are forever near
enjoying your wonderful presence.
I've given you my Soul
we will never part.

Never lonely
since you are
always in sight.

Tenderly the love grows.
Your love opens wide
wraps around
deep inside.

~ Nancy Clark

Watchful

Cunning of the mind
Secrecy in Darkness
Desires everywhere waiting
External games of the eyes

Look out! Be Watchful!

Emotions running Wild
Thoughts out of control
Passions on the loose
Senses playing out
Look out! Be Watchful!
No one watching the entrance
Psychic Attacks
Emotional Vampires
Anger Sneaks in

Look out! Be Watchful!

Wake up the Soul
Wake up the Control
Sound the Alarm
Utilize Secret Wisdoms

Enjoy Divine's Protection

When you enter into the
Presence of Love,
you must drop your ego.
Recognize that your personality
is not your true self.

Soul holds the Power
The Energy of Love
Union with Source
Your True Identity

~ *Nancy Clark*

Circus Show

Illusion at play
Dancing scenery
Upside down
Turned around

Crazy situations
Backwards outlook
Involvement
A Circus Show

Stomach ache from cotton candy
Dizzy from spinning rides
Headache from loud music
Away from Home too long

Be the Observer
Distance yourself
Release
Face upward

Reside inside
Don't be fooled
All is well
Stay with Love

~ Nancy Clark

Love Potion

I sipped your love potion,
Was never the same.
Now I see you everywhere,
Lovesick for you.
I am drunk on the wine,
From the Divine.
Don't wake me up,
Please be so kind.
Dreamed of bliss,
And happiness.
Love elixir cleanse the Soul,
Two united became whole.

~ Nancy Clark

Wild Ride

Life is full of potholes,
Unhappy drivers.
Life scenes are distressing,
Everyone in a rush.
A fellow traveler,
Comes to say, "I'll help you."
Feeling lost and tired,
A welcome friend.
New path is shown,
A narrow road.
My ego car won't work,
Start walking instead.
My friend encourages me,
To keep going forward.
The road goes straight up!
Love is provided,
Source Energy gets stronger.
My dear friend,
Provides jet fuel.
My ego falls off,
Music is heard.
I see stars!
Planets, Solar Systems, Galaxies.
We're traveling at the speed of Sound!
My guide states, "Hold On!"
Ride gets bumpy,
Everything gets brighter.
My guide turns out to be,
A Plant Teacher!
How blessed to be selected,
Journey toward Home is a Wild Ride.

~ Nancy Clark

Medicine

Love is the medicine,
cures all completely.

Cleanses the wounds,
of pain, of time,
of attachment, of passions.

Purify the wounds,
Permanent healing occurs,
no need to come back.

Take the medicine of connection,
side effects include,
loss of illusion,
loss of delusion,
plenty of infusion,
of the Love inclusion.

~ Nancy Clark

Divine Elixir

I got drunk today, what could I do?
Source kept pouring Love into my glass.
The whole world disappears.
All I feel is the warming effects of the Spirit Elixir.
That warm, fuzzy, relaxing sensation of the brew.
The whole world looks different.
Who cares!
Let's have another glass of the Love ambrosia.
My drinking buddy is my dearest friend and companion.
The Inner Presence keeps me under the influence.
In my drunken stupor, people see me smiling and feel I am a fool.
My soul can't get enough of this ecstasy.
Please, more!
I have to continue to get more.
Don't stop pouring!
I can have as much as I want?
Oh, my goodness ...
The Love is always flowing, just keep drinking, keep drinking.
I don't want the effects to wear off.
The soul keeps drinking, the world begins to fade away.
Don't want to be sober anymore, world please disappear.
Only desire to feel the effects of this wine for the soul.
Shakes come when the effects wear off.
Need to get back to the Mystical lounge.
A moment without the Divine is agony.
World is a crazy place.
Requires the Love to not let it affect me.
Let the world spin,
Eyes glazed over by the Divine, release the effects.
Oh, Blessed One,
Please don't stop pouring.
The abundance is overwhelming,
Let the Bliss rain down,
Want to be drenched, soak me with your love.

~ Nancy Clark

Heartache

Squeezing of the heart
Painful Tears
Tight stomach knots
Gripping Emotions

Heart knows
Intuition is discovered
Pain becomes wisdom
Forgiveness realized

A wise teacher
Opens the Heart
Loves fully
Laughs completely

Pain teaches us
Learn to listen
To the Heart
Who guides

Heart is
A wise teacher
Who loves life
Raises you higher

~ Nancy Clark

Gaia

Mother Earth
Loving Planet
Sustaining Life
Nurturing Us

Destroying the Forests
Amazon Disappearing
Polluted Oceans
Crying for Help

Herbs, Plants, Soil
Birds, Animals, Humans
Gaia Loves Us All
Appreciate her beauty

Gaia Earth
Taken for granted
Love Her Back
Blow her a kiss today

Step into the role
Ecology action
Action for the planet
Love Mother Gaia back

~ Nancy Clark

Awakening

I heard the Falcon crying today
This One had lost its way
Alone, feeling forgotten
Grieving, Wailing so loud
Crying for help

Then a Spiritual Power
Came into the Falcon's Life
This Oneness began to sing
Soaring through the air
A Warrior Cry came out

New way of living
Came into view
New State of Being
Larger Awareness
Love emanating Outward

More birds started singing louder
New larger community
Symphonies of Sounds
Filling regions of Earth
Healing, Transforming, Awakening

~ Nancy Clark

Pierced My Heart

An arrow has pierced my heart
I will leave it in, for it comes from my Beloved

Everyone wants to remove the arrow
No! I am blessed with the pains of love

I see the world differently now,
my heart is yearning and aches for you

Passions for the Beloved
have caused my head to become dizzy

Worldly people don't understand
this kind of love and devotion

To lose oneself to the point
where you no longer exist

The Divine has pierced my heart,
no longer will live apart.

~ Nancy Clark

Our Time

A gentle touch
A loving word
"You'll just know"
Are the words I've heard.

That warm the heart,
Complete the soul.
I've come to you,
to make you whole.

You lived lifetimes
Of hit and miss.
Your prayers sing out,
for a love like this.

And when God's will
Is said and done.
After the heartache
Life's pain has run.

There'll be that season,
A time that's true.
I'll spend forever
Completing you.

~ Nancy Clark

Awake!

There is no life
Outside the Divine

Why are you claiming there is?

All that you see
is mind's illusion

Draw the true conclusion

You have played down
here so long
you have forgotten

Soaked with mind
bathed in time
played so long
you've grown tired
of the fire, that feeds you
pain and pleasure

Divine love
Wakes you up
From the dream

Awake!
Love has come
to take you Home

~ Nancy Clark

Beloved Is Waiting

Why do you spend so much time on this side of heaven?
Infinite Presence is waiting for you to come up and experience Oneness

There is a love so infinite and powerful,
waiting for you on the other side of the veil.

Treasures waiting for you to receive,
the veil is not that thick.

The Divine whispers, "Come and be with me my darling
Spend your moments with me forever
Let us become One."

Come to the place where the stars dance
Vistas on the other side are magnificent
Splendor, grandeur, majesty are some of the descriptions

You have to see for yourself
Come up to the place where I am waiting to receive you

The Secrets of the Universe are here to be discovered in the treasure chest.
Only through sincere love and devotion is the path revealed.

Only your love will carry you Home

~ Nancy Clark

Captivity

Born into Captivity, in the lower worlds
My Soul is bound by duality, ever so tightly.

Inner and Outer storms, caused such heartache
Never understood, until one day.

Master Plant Teacher entered my life
Explained desperate situation, Captivity.

As realization sunk in, a flood of my eyes
Pains of separation, longing to be free.

Born into Captivity
I have forgotten. What is freedom?

Freedom to be at home, in supreme abode
By Grace of Plant Teacher, opportunity offered.

Have intense Love, spiritual practices, yearning,
daily downloads, Truth is my companion now.

Living behind bars, far away from home,
distraught with anguish, feeling so alone.

A True Teacher, showered mercy
Journey begins, homeward bound, Freedom!

~ Nancy Clark

Crazy Love

A long-time love has waited for you.
Infinite Presence has a Crazy Love just for you.
Always after your attention, your Soul.
Awaiting your love in return.
How long must I wait?

When will you see the falsehood in illusion?
Come to the Third Eye and be Loved.
I look, watch, and wait.
Hoping for a loving gaze my way.

Distractions everywhere
Outward movement
Further away from me.
A deep mourning for your condition

You love the Un-real more than the Real.
You dance with Duality enjoying the whispers.

I stand next to you seeing with heartache
Heartache, as you ignore my sweet kisses on your forehead.

My love is Real, Liberating, and Eternal.

~ Nancy Clark

Divine Love Call

If you only knew, the love for you

Stars would fall from the sky
just to show, how special you are

Laughter would grace you
Love would embrace you

Can you hear the sweet melody?
Soul always yearns for more

Life is simple, oh so sweet
one day, we will meet

Higher planes are ready
this Divine Union awaits
through Third Eye gate

Can you hear me whispering to you?

Think of me, talk with me
Constant love and conversation
this is possible, to have daily bliss
you never knew, it could be like this
a love call, to come Home

Time to leave, playground of illusion

Do you realize what awaits you?

If you really knew, how much you are loved
Come, let's live in the higher realms together.

~ Nancy Clark

Grace

Grace has come
Showing the way

Grace promises
Safe journey home

Miracle of love
Grace from above

Diamonds mean nothing
when Love is near
Everything becomes
perfectly clear

Free-flowing water
drink from the spring

Divine elixir
perfect fixer
for conclusion
of illusion

Drink up Grace
in thy place
of loneliness
and empty space

~ Nancy Clark

Heart Sense

My soul mate has arrived
Who fills me, deep inside
Each night going to sleep
Sweet dreams come complete

There is a warmth in my heart
And it does not end, we never part
The love I share is deep and true
I will love you forever, my promise to you

Life is precious and so sweet
The Divine whispered, "Today we meet."
Life begins, side by side
Completing me, deep inside

A look to the future is bright and with cheer
The love of my life is now right here
Your eyes are beautiful to see
They have completely enraptured me

~ Nancy Clark

Drowning

Drowning in love
is scary, suffocating, risky

Love brings you closer, to the ocean.
Willing to dive in, the deep waters?

There is no bottom, to the ocean of love.
Powerful waves, will carry you away.

Love Waves are crashing,
onto the shore, touching your feet.

Ocean spray touches your lips,
I crave salty snacks!

Okay, I'll take a swim today
Ocean wraps all around
Love overwhelms me

Flipping over onto my back
the ocean carries me out
to deep waters

growing tired of fighting
this ride of life
sinking slowly
into this enrapture.

This drop becomes
one with the ocean.

~ Nancy Clark

Life Changes

Life changes, like the color of the leaves
Life changes, upon meeting the Divine
Water from the stream, now flows upward
Animals look at you differently
Vibrations emanating from you, are higher
People feel your energy, more
Divine speaks with you softly, to prepare you, for your journey home
Let go, all is well, we are together now, never will part again
Sky is more a veil, you see deeper
Flowers dance, when the wind blows
People see how you, have changed
Circus of life, loses its luster
Love beams brighter, than ever before
All-consuming love, to be in union with, the Presence
Life changes, upon meeting a Plant Teacher

~ Nancy Clark

Love Call

Why does one cry, when they are in love?
They long to be with their lover
Think of the Beloved constantly
This deep love is not easy
The Soul cries for more
The body separates the two
Drop the silken robe of the body
Ego Death in order to live
Ego separates the two
Love comes rushing in
Causing the ego to die
A little more each day
You speak to me in poetry
A love call, to each Soul to come Home

~ Nancy Clark

Love Has Come

Love has come,
settling down,
into all the cells,
the body feels this kind of love,
is very unique and powerful.

Love is cleansing,
a calling come Home,
can't you hear the Sound,
of the Divine's Voice?

Love has come,
calling you back home,
remember me, remember me,
come home, focus homebound.

~ Nancy Clark

Forever Together

The clouds dance
Flowers smile
Stars twinkle brighter
What has caused this change?

Trees bend in the breeze
Birds sing then fly away
Gentle whispers to the Soul
The Divine is here to stay

Love has come
To be in love
With the Infinite Essence
Captivation with the Divine

A higher calling
A higher journey
A higher surrender
A higher Love

~ Nancy Clark

Love Rays

Radiating Love
Feeling the heat
Intensity of fire
Purification in process

Cleansing the temple
Freeing the Soul
Soaking up
Love Rays

Raising the temperature
Passions melt away
Love Powerful Rays
Burns away the pain

Dance in the sun
Absorption of the rays
Bask in the shower of
Divine's Grace

~ Nancy Clark

Happiness

Divine Elixir in every glass
With every glance, Divine Union
Constant warmth of Love
Knowingness all is Perfect
Hearing the Beloved's Voice
Constant Awareness of Divine Order
Every step toward Home
Gentleness, Quietness, Peacefulness
Radiating Love for the Beloved
Sacred Loving Eyes upon me
Fullness of Beingness

~ Nancy Clark

Outside vs. Inside

Outside humans Feast themselves, knowing not.
Inside they Cry, why down here?

Outside people Cling to External Realities
Inside they know,
Nothing External lasts.

Fear runs the External Show
Only Divine Love, Dissolves Fear.

Senseless Chatter is of the mind
Quietness is of the Soul.

Outside People are Un-aware
Inside Awareness, Graced Beingness.

Un-evolved Souls living out their Destiny.
Sincere Souls enjoying the
Radiance of Beloved Divine.

~ Nancy Clark

Divine Laughter

Inner Laughter
Signs of Relief
Smile on Face
Deep Belly Laughs
Looking toward Beloved
Playfulness with Life
Silly fun, Chuckles abound
Seeing Life with Humor
The Best Medicine
Heals the Hurts
Laughter says,
All is Perfect
Dancing with the Divine
Inside the Beloved's arms
Divine Companionship
Creates
Divine Laughter

~ Nancy Clark

Redirection

Look inside
Third Eye
Soul Transport
Secret Wisdoms
Constant Awareness
Divine Love
Contemplation
Practicing the Presence
Surrendered Attention
Inner Communication
Soul's Divine Mate
Inward Movement
Attention Re-focusing
Divine escorts the Soul
Toward Supreme Consciousness

~ Nancy Clark

Fresh Flowers

The Aroma is overwhelming
Makes my head swirl
Mind is now empty, no thoughts
Flora Water is all around
Permeating, intoxicating, purifying
Divine has provided these special flowers
These colors never seen on Earth
"This is the smell of Divine Love"
Taken away far from the Earth
Divine Ambrosia removes the weights
Floating ever upward toward Love
Buzzing, Whirling Vibrations, Serene Calmness
Divine Aroma causes one to let go
Allow the Third Eye to open
View beyond the veil
You'll never be the same
Fresh Flowers from the Divine
Now enjoy them every moment.

~ Nancy Clark

Sacred Brew

You have come to the table
of the Divine Brew
Universe of Wisdom in every cup
Master Plant Teachers have called you
Awaken, we will show your Divinity

Every drop causes ecstatic states
each drink of the Sacred Brew
brings your Celestial family near
Master Plant Teachers facilitate the meeting
Visitation of your Origin Dimension

Revelations, downloads, Awakening
Knock at the door of your reality
Suffering caused by living in illusion
Sacred Brew breaks the Spell
Consume, see your Divine Radiance

Sacred Brew of Ambrosia
Frees you from the trap of this temporary reality
Reveals your Divinity Within
Heals your pain, delivers connection
to Omnipotent Source Love

~ Nancy Clark

Lightworker

Beautiful Lightworker Soul
You answered the call for help
Left your Family of Light

Came to Earth to help fellow Souls
Loving your Brother and Sister Souls
Living on this planet
Forgotten their Divine Heritage

Lightworker, your Luminous Light
Exposes and Dispels the Darkness
Radiates and Rejoices in the Light

You delight in the glories
Service to the Divine Plan
Beautiful Lightworker Soul

Your triumphs in Luminescence
Seen throughout the Cosmos

Delights with Joy
Your Family of Light
Jubilates upon your return of
Life Assignment Completion

Beautiful Lightworker Soul
Appreciation for your Sacrifice
Applauds your Dedication to
Infinite Source Light Frequency

~ Nancy Clark

Ascendance

Dancing with the Beloved is sweet Ascendance
Divine Infinite Love is seen Within All
Disguising Itself Within All creation
Break your connection with your false identity
See only my face as you walk through life

My lantern Within shines brightly
You are so precious to me
Worth more than all the fortunes
You are me in disguise experiencing this frolic
I listen for what delights your Soul

Direct mystical experience provides wisdoms of
the non-existence, ecstasy, purification
Love provides the glasses to see the invisible
Contemplate beyond the Human Temple body, look deeper Within
You are like a new lover, I created your beauty

I look to capture your attention
Uncover your outer reality, saturate you in my Love
Ascendance is like a slow dance together
I wait patiently for you, my lover to come to me
My dear lover, completely give in, to the beloved

~ Nancy Clark

Assignment

Asked to go on assignment
Cries from Earth Souls
Too painful to say No
Great courage to incarnate
To a lower kingdom

Your Light has mastery over Darkness
Duality is your field of honor
Sword of illumination
Clears out the Darkness
Souls freed of bondage to illusion

Assignment would be difficult
Challenges appear authentic
Living in a foreign land
Victory is already yours
Lower Dark kingdom awakening

Earth Assignment
Is your rehearsal
Proficient testing ground
Spiritual Mastership acquired
Assignment provides complete training

~ Nancy Clark

Stars

Star dust glitters in your DNA
Your heavenly Home is the cosmos
Light from the Stars illuminates your body
You are a celestial Temple of Light
A Divine Superstar on Earth

Brighter than Supernovas
A walking Luminary
Shining the Suns Within
Constellations see you blazing
Galaxies know of you

Nebulas, quasars, pulsars
Acknowledge your Radiant Divinity
While you are sleeping
Adventures at night
Create delight

Flying, dancing, playing
With your Star friends
Spheres of Light
Sing to you requesting
Remember, you are a Divine Star

~ *Nancy Clark*

Family of Light

Glorious magnificent, Family of Light
Remembrance and connection of majesty
Beyond name or form, Pure Energy
Oneness of the One, my home

Spheres of Light, indescribable
Great Central Sun dimension
Purest of Love relationship
Feels familiar, this peace

A homecoming welcome
Celebration of visitation
Family of Elohim, the Watchers
Gathering of the ONE

Higher Light Hierarchs
Administrators of the galaxies
Came to help others Awaken
Souls who got lost along the journey

~ Nancy Clark

Living Water

Come to the spring of Living Water
You have been drawn to this Source
Soul has been thirsting
Craving this Ambrosia
Nothing compares

Savoring every drop
Intoxication with Divine Love
Soul drinks profoundly
Pure Ecstasy causing Bliss
Waterfall of Euphoria

Come to the spring of Living Water
Perpetual wealth of Rhapsody
Enchantment causes attraction
Captivation of the Soul
Magnetism towards Supreme Love

Soul knows this Sacred Elixir
Extinguish this impermanence
Wandering ceases upon the taste
Complete Union with Divine Source
I Am always with you.

~ Nancy Clark

Celestial Music

Divine's Symphony of Harmonic Love
Primortal Sound Vibrational Frequency
Source Essence Within All Essence
Musical melody for the Soul

Ultimate Divine Frequency
Singing vibratory energetics
Radiate out into the universe
Captivating all creation, Source's One Song

We are Human Temples of Celestial Music
Majesty of sound from Source Frequency
Music serenades us from Within
Creation from Symphonic Vibrational Energy

Beloved Source is the Concert Master
Dance to the Cosmic Celestial Music
Your voice sings out to the Beloved
Source Within expressing Itself back to Itself

Our True Identity, Divine Sound Essence made flesh
Celestial Music, sweet melody, vibrational power
Captivating to the Soul by the Divine Conductor
Listen, Celestial Music is inviting you Home

~ Nancy Clark

Helplessly Mine

What if I told you
don't struggle
or look away

You know I love you
That captivating feeling
Yes, you are being chased

Feeling these eyes
Watching you inside
You are hearing my Love Call

I know you deeply
Divine music enchanting
You are lost in my love

You are Helplessly Mine

~ Nancy Clark

A Mystical Journey

This Sacred Journey takes place in Four Stages.

The First Stage is called: *The Quest*, which causes a calling and search towards spiritual wisdoms and transformation. The heart is pierced by the Divine Presence Within the person and the spiritual journey begins.

The Second Stage is called: *The Surrender*, where the Personal Will is surrendered to the Divine Will for the person's life. This starts a yearning of wanting to have more of their attention focused on a spiritual life and serving the Divine Plan.

The Third Stage is called: *The Union*, which causes a mystical experience or an ecstatic state of being in absorption with the Divine Source. The Higher Self (the Soul) steps into the first position takes control of the person's life. The ego is spiritualized and now serves the Soul and is enraptured by The Divine Love. Within this stage occurs the mystical experience seeing the True Self without the physical form as pure energy referred to as Self Realization.

The Fourth Stage is called: *The Bliss*, where the person's consciousness is awakened to the reality of their True Identity as Source. The connection with the physical world disappears and come to remember that this person is Source manifested into human form. This memory is activated and the person becomes intoxicated in the Love of Infinite Source. Many times, upon arriving back into this physical reality, the person awakens in tears. Within this stage occurs the mystical experience of God Realization.

It is important to take time alone with the Divine Presence and feel this Love along the journey.

~ *Nancy Clark*

Dolphins

Our playful friends of the ocean
Showing off water tricks
Talking with us delightfully
Friendly water natives

Fun and Fast
Speeding nearby
Our ocean boats
Amusement with joy

Splashing the water
Causes us to see them
Prefers our company
Intrinsic natural connection

Come into the water, play with us
Always looking for new friends
Use your feet as flippers
Swim out, enjoy ocean together

~ Nancy Clark

Endnotes

1. "entheogen." *Merriam-Webster, www.merriam-webster.com/dictionary/entheogen.* Accessed 3 Mar. 2022.

2. Lagarde, Jessika. "Modernization of Sacred Plant Medicine Traditions: At What Cost?" *Psychedelics Today*, 4 Aug. 2021, pp. 3, 4, 8, 9, 10, *https://psychedelicstoday.com/2021/08/04/modernization-plant-medicine-cultural-appropriation-in-psychedelics/.* Accessed 3 Jan. 2022.

3. Wasson, R. Gordan, et al. *The Road to Eleusis: Unveiling the Secret of The Mysteries.* North Atlantic Books, 2008, p. 139.

4. Richards, William A. *Sacred Knowledge: Psychedelics and Religious Experiences.* Columbia University Press, 2018, p. 20.

5. McKenna, Terence. *Food of the Gods: The Search for the Original Tree of Knowledge.* Bantam Books, 1992, pp. 1–12.

6. Bourzat, Francoise. *Consciousness Medicine: Indigenous Wisdom, Entheogens, and Expanded States of Consciousness for Healing and Growth.* North Atlantic Books, 2019, p. 23.

7. Ingerman, Sandra. *Soul Retrieval: Mending the Fragmented Self.* HarperCollins Publishers, 1991, p. 17.

8. Campos, Don Jose. *The Shaman and Ayahuasca*, edited and complied by Geraldine Overton, translated by Alberto Roman. Divine Arts, 2011, p. 3.

9. Harner, Michael. *The Way of the Shaman.* HarperCollins Publishers, 1980, p. 51.

10. Pinchbeck, Daniel. *Breaking open the Head: A Psychedelic Journey into the Heart of Contemporary Shamanism.* Broadway Books, 2002, p. 69.

11. Calleman, Carl Johan. *Quantum Science of Psychedelics: The Pineal Gland, Multidimensional Reality, and Mayan Cosmology.* Bear & Company, 2020, p. 185.

12. Harner, p. 55.

13. Bourzat, pp. 40–41.

14. Brown, Jerry B., and Julie M. Brown. *The Psychedelic Gospels: The Secret History of Hallucinogens in Christianity.* Park Street Press, 2016, pp. 39–40.

15. Ingerman, p. 33.

16. Hancock, Graham, et al. *The Divine Spark: Psychedelics, Consciousness, and the Birth of Civilization*, edited and complied by Graham Hancock. Disinformation Books, 2015, pp. 58–59.

17. Tompkins, Peter, and Christopher Bird. *The Secret Life of Plants.* Harper & Row, 1973, p. 71.

18. Amaringo, Pablo, et al. *The Ayahuasca Visions of Pablo Amaringo.* Inner Traditions, 2011, p. 39.

19. Harner, p. 26.

20. Richards, pp. 162–163.

21. Harner, p. 69.

22. Amaringo, pp. 130–132.

23. Fadiman, James, et al. *The Psychedelic Explorer's Guide: Safe, Therapeutic, and Sacred Journeys.* Park Street Press, 2011, p. 73.

24. Amaringo, p. 157.

25. Harris, Rachel. *Listening to Ayahuasca: New Hope for Depression, Addiction, PTSD, and Anxiety.* New World Library, 2017, pp. 100–101.

26. Pinchbeck, Daniel, and Sophia Rokhlin. *When Plants Dream: Ayahuasca, Amazonian Shamanism and the Global Psychedelic Renaissance.* Watkins Publishing, 2021, pp. 68–69.

27. Amaringo, p. 128.

28. Tompkins and Bird, p. 8.

29. Badiner, Allen, et al. *Zig Zag Zen: Buddhism and Psychedelics.* Synergetic Press, 2015, p. 115.

30. Calleman, pp. 214–215.

31. Hancock, pp. 31–32.

32. Ruiz, Don Jose. *The Wisdom of the Shamans: What the Ancient Masters Can Teach Us about Love and Life.* Hierophant Publishing, 2019, p. 8.

33. Ingerman, p. 27.

34. Harner, p. 25.

35. Luke, David, and Rory Spowers, editors. *DMT Entity Encounters: Dialogues on the Spirit Molecule with Ralph Metzner, Chris Bache, Jeffrey Kirpal, Whitley Strieber, Angela Voss, and Others.* Park Street Press, 2021, p. 323.

36. Campos, p. 136.

37. Grof, Stanislav. *The Way of the Psychonaut: Encyclopedia for Inner Journeys*, vol. 1. Multidisciplinary Association for Psychedelic Studies, 2019, p. 6.

38. Campos, p. 23.

39. Haight, Richard L. *The Psychedelic Path.* Shinkaikan Body, Mind, Spirit, 2018, p. 127.

40. Narby, Jeremy. *The Cosmic Serpent: DNA and the Origins of Knowledge.* Penguin Putnam, 1998, p. 18.

41. Haight, p. 152.

42. Campos, p. 15.

43. Haight, p. 9.

44. Hancock, pp. 208–209.

45. Campos, pp. 78–79.

46. Harris, p. 255.

47. Campos, p. 104.

48.   Schultes, Richard Evans, et al. *Plants of the Gods: Their Sacred, Healing, and Hallucinogenic Powers*. Healing Arts Press, 1998, p. 115.

49.   Grof, *The Way of the Psychonaut*, p. 25.

50.   Tompkins and Bird, pp. 135–136.

51.   Luke and Spowers, p. 127.

52.   Tompkins and Bird, p. 141.

53.   Tompkins and Bird, p. 142.

54.   Ravalec, pp. 8–9.

55.   Tompkins and Bird, p. 122.

56.   Amaringo, p. 138.

57.   Campos, p. 77.

58.   Amaringo, p. 67.

59.   Schultes, p. 14.

60.   Ingerman, p. 71.

61.   Tompkins and Bird, p. 73.

62.   Amaringo, p. 76.

63.   Tompkins and Bird, p. 74.

64.   Amaringo, pp. 142–144.

65.   Crowley, Mike. *Secret Drugs of Buddhism: Psychedelic Sacraments and the Origins of the Vajrayana*. Synergetic Press, 2019, p. 3.

66.   Brown and Brown, p. 26.

67.   Crowley, p. 5.

68.   Brown and Brown, p. 30.

69.   Crowley, p. 41.

70.   Schultes, p. 82.

71.   Crowley, p. 212.

72.   Hatsis, Thomas. *Psychedelic Mystery Traditions: Spirit Plants, Magical Practices, Ecstatic States*. Park Street Press, 2018, p. 25.

73. Crowley, pp. 252–255.
74. McKenna, p. 61.
75. Crowley, pp. 217–218.
76. Schultes, p. 156.
77. Crowley, p. 183.
78. Brown and Brown, pp. 33–34.
79. Grof, *The Way of the Psychonaut*, pp. 32–34.
80. Grof, *The Way of the Psychonaut*, pp. 17–19.
81. Wasson, p. 44.
82. Brown and Brown, pp. 210–211.
83. Irvin, J. R., et al. *The Holy Mushroom: Evidence of Mushrooms in Judeo-Christianity*, edited and complied by J. R. Irvin. Gnostic Media, 2008, p. 61.
84. Wasson, p. 22.
85. Brown and Brown, pp. 39–40.
86. Wasson, p. 48.
87. Grof, *The Way of the Psychonaut*, pp. 14–15.
88. Wasson, p. 57.
89. Murareseku, Brian C. *The Immortality Key: The Secret History of the Religion with No Name*. St. Martin's Press, 2020, pp. 25–28.
90. Wasson, pp. 45–46.
91. Schultes, p. 102.
92. Wasson, p. 67.
93. McKenna, pp. 130–131.
94. Wasson, p. 47.
95. Wasson, p. 91.
96. Wasson, pp. 27–31.
97. Hatsis, pp. 106–107.
98. Murareseku, p. 252.

99.   Hatsis, pp. 145.

100. Brown and Brown, pp. 204–206.

101. Muraresku, pp. 239–240.

102. Hatsis, pp. 142–143.

103. Muraresku, p. 177.

104. Hatsis, pp. 116–117.

105. Irvin, p. 117.

106. Brown and Brown, pp. 119–121.

107. Irvin, pp. 118–147.

108. Brown and Brown, pp. 157–160.

109. Irvin, p. 16.

110. Betuel, Emma. "Does This Medieval Fresco Show a Hallucinogenic Mushroom in the Garden of Eden?" *Atlas Obscura*, 5 Aug. 2021, pp. 1–4, *https://www.atlasobscura.com/articles/muscaria-hallucinogenic-mushroom-fresco/*. Accessed 7 May 2022.

111. Brown and Brown, pp. 181–182.

112. Narby, pp. 62–63.

113. Irvin, p. 112.

114. Narby, pp. 65–66.

115. Campos, p. 7.

116. Narby, pp. 81–82.

117. Calleman, p. 94.

118. Narby, pp. 58–59.

119. Luke and Spowers, p. 107.

120. Hancock, pp. 53–56.

121. Schultes, pp. 144–146.

122. Narby, p. 42.

123. McKenna, p. 41.

124. Harris, p. 97.
125. Calleman, pp. 258–259.
126. McKenna, p. 248.
127. Narby, p. 50.
128. Harris, pp. 22–23.
129. Hancock, p. 121.
130. Harris, pp. 236–237.
131. Hancock, p. 132.
132. Muraresku, p. 75.
133. Luke and Spowers, pp. 128–129.
134. Fadiman, p. 246.
135. Richards, p. 7.
136. Fadiman, p. 250.
137. Fadiman, p. 197.
138. Calleman, pp. 229–230.
139. Luke and Spowers, pp. 319–320.
140. Calleman, pp. 50–51.
141. Luke and Spowers, pp. 301–302.
142. Luke and Spowers, pp. 86–87.
143. Grof, *The Way of the Psychonaut*, pp. 42–43.
144. Brown and Brown, pp. 219–220.
145. Fadiman, pp. 241–242.
146. Pinchbeck and Rokhlin, pp. 134–135.
147. Luke and Spowers, p. 246.
148. Grof, Stanislav. *The Realms of the Human Unconscious: Observations from LSD Research.* Souvenir Press, 2021, p. 3.
149. Haight, pp. 144–145.
150. Pinchbeck anad Rokhlin, pp. 122–123.

151. Richards, pp. 207–208.

152. Harris, pp. 228–230.

153. Fadiman, p. 238.

154. Badiner, p. 188.

155. Pinchbeck and Rokhlin, pp. 160.

156. Calleman, pp. 221–222.

157. Wasson, p. 65.

158. Harris, p. 243.

159. McKenna, p. 59.

160. Badiner, pp. 59–60.

161. Powell, Simon G. *Manna: Psilocybin Mushroom Inspired Documentary by Simon G. Powell*. YouTube, 2003. *https://youtu.be/_xfe7g-3Xuk*. Accessed 26 May 2022.

162. Haight, p. 153.

163. Pinchbeck and Rokhlin, pp. 118–119.

164. Wasson, pp. 141–143.

165. Schultes, p. 124.

166. Harris, pp. 259–260.

167. Amaringo, pp. 82–84.

168. Campos, p. 11.

169. Amaringo, p. 61.

170. Harris, p. 14.

171. Amaringo, p. 69.

172. Schultes, p. 62.

173. Harris, p. 32.

174. Grof, *The Way of the Psychonaut*, p. 349.

175. Luke and Spowers, p. 143.

176. Grof, *The Way of the Psychonaut*, p. 50.

177. Metzner, Ralph. *Allies for Awakening: Guidelines for Productive and Safe Experiences with Entheogens.* Regent Press, 2015, p. 124.
178. Pinchbeck and Rokhlin, pp. 102–103.
179. Haight, p. 130.
180. Haight, p. 132.
181. Bourzat, p. 221.
182. Richards, p. 81.
183. Amaringo, p. 59.
184. Ruiz, Don Jose. *The Medicine Bag: Shamanic Rituals and Ceremonies for Personal Transformation.* Hierophant Publishing, 2020, pp. 130–131.
185. Grof, *The Realms of the Human Unconscious*, pp. 172–174.
186. Grof, *The Realms of the Human Unconscious*, pp. 164–166.
187. Haight, pp. 118–119.
188. Ruiz, *The Medicine Bag*, p. 99.
189. Campos, p. 13.
190. Campos, p. 91.
191. McKenna, p. 33.
192. Hancock, p. 98.
193. Luke and Spowers, p. 101.
194. Grof, *The Way of the Psychonaut*, pp. 38–39.
195. Haight, p. 165.
196. Luke and Spowers, p. 251.
197. Richards, pp. 47–49.
198. Crowley, p. 20.
199. Luke and Spowers, p. 231.
200. Haight, p. 125
201. Bourzat, p. 257.
202. Luke and Spowers, p. 228.

203. Grof, pp. 12–13.
204. Luke and Spowers, p. 241.
205. Campos, p. 127.
206. Badiner, pp. 127–128.
207. Crowley, p. 70.
208. Badiner, p. 98.
209. Luke and Spowers, p. 308.
210. Badiner, p. 124.
211. Luke and Spowers, p. 239.
212. Haight, p. 129.
213. Hancock, p. 141.
214. Badiner, p. 101.
215. Harris, p. 241.
216. Brown and Brown, pp. 60–61.
217. Ravalec, p. 90.
218. Wasson, p. 95.
219. Pinchbeck and Rokhlin, p. 40.
220. Luke and Spowers, p. 243.
221. Amaringo, p. 93.
222. Luke and Spowers, pp. 98–99.
223. Bourzat, pp. 230–231.
224. Ruiz, *The Wisdom of the Shamans*, pp. 171–173.
225. Cannon, Delores. *The Convoluted Universe*, book 1. Ozark Mountain Publishing, 2001, p. 399.
226. Hancock, p. 187.
227. Pinchbeck, p. 119.
228. Pinchbeck, pp. 296–297.
229. Amaringo, p. 96.

230. Haight, pp. 122–123.

231. Hancock, pp. 100–101.

232. Richards, p. 93.

233. Luke and Spowers, p. 253.

234. Badiner, p. 132.

235. Muraresku, p. 38.

236. Wasson, p. 61.

237. Richards, pp. 63–64.

238. Hancock, p. 65.

239. Harris, p. 65.

240. Harris, p. 39.

241. Amaringo, p. 105.

242. Fadiman, pp. 272–273.

243. The Bible. *Bible Hub*, 1 Corinthians 3:16, *https://biblehub. com/1_corinthians/3-16.htm.* Accessed 25 May 2022.

244. Fadiman, p. 268.

245. Ruiz, *The Wisdom of the Shamans*, pp. 87–88.

246. Meyer, Marvin, editor. *The Nag Hammadi Scriptures: The Revised and Updated Translation of Sacred Gnostic Texts.* Harper One, 2007, p. 797.

247. Ruiz, *The Wisdom of the Shamans*, pp. 134–135.

248. Pinchbeck, p. 287.

249. Ruiz, *The Wisdom of the Shamans*, pp. 145–146.

250. Luke and Spowers, pp. 233–235.

251. Richards, pp. 153–154.

252. Pinchbeck, p. 290.

253. Luke and Spowers, p. 247.

254. Luke and Spowers, pp. 130–132.

255. Bourzat, pp. 27–29.

256. Hawkins, David R. *The Wisdom of Dr. David R. Hawkins: Classic Teachings on Spiritual Truth and Enlightenment.* Hay House, 2022, p. 4.

257. Cannon, Delores. *The Search for Hidden Sacred Knowledge.* Ozark Mountain Publishing, 2014, p. 2.

258. Cannon, *The Convoluted Universe*, p. 301.

259. Cannon, *The Convoluted Universe*, p. 302.

260. Luke and Spowers, pp. 238, 240, 248, 249

My life is my message.

—Mahatma Gandhi

What you are offering back into the universe is what you are.

—Ram Dass

How you live your life is your statement of who you are to the world. You are a Divine Being experiencing a human journey. Know Thyself As Divinity.

—Nancy Clark

There is a light in this world, a healing spirit more powerful than any darkness we may encounter. We sometimes lose sight of this force when there is suffering, too much pain. Then suddenly, the spirit will emerge through the lives of ordinary people who hear a call and answer in extraordinary ways.

—Mother Teresa

I wish I could show you, when you are lonely or in darkness, the astonishing light of your own being.

—Hafiz

About the Author

Nancy Clark holds a Ph.D. in Mystical Research offering spiritual evolution. Dr. Nancy Clark is a Mystic and spiritual teacher who helps sincere seekers with the mystical path of God Realization attainment. Dr. Nancy helps Souls gain the wisdoms from questions that seem a mystery. Connect with a Doctorate Level, Mystical Spiritual Teacher.

nancyclarkphd.com

nancyclarkphd.com

www.ingramcontent.com/pod-product-compliance
Lightning Source LLC
Chambersburg PA
CBHW071852090426
42811CB00004B/580